# Modern Politics

### C.L.R. James

*Modern Politics*
C.L.R. James

This edition © 2013 PM Press
All rights reserved. No part of this book may be transmitted by any means
without permission in writing from the publisher.

PM Press
PO Box 23912
Oakland, CA 94623
www.pmpress.org

Published in conjunction with the Charles H. Kerr Publishing Company
C.H. Kerr Company
1726 Jarvis Avenue
Chicago, IL 60626
www.charleshkerr.com

Cover design by Josh MacPhee/justseeds.org/antumbradesign.org
Interior design by Jonathan Rowland/briandesign

ISBN: 978–1–60486–311–6
LCCN: 2012955002

10 9 8 7 6 5 4 3 2

Printed in the USA

# Contents

# Introduction
## By Noel Ignatiev

MODERN POLITICS CONSISTS of a series of lectures C.L.R. James delivered in 1960 at the Adult Education Center in Port of Spain, Trinidad.[1] During his twenty-five-year absence from his native land, James had become known to a few in the radical movement as the founder and leader of a distinctive current of Marxism and more widely as a writer on sports, history, philosophy and culture, and had been recognized as one of the pioneers of West Indian independence.[2] The lectures are a survey of Western civilization. Why did James, a black man who knew the crimes of the West firsthand, speaking to a mostly black audience of colonials, choose to lecture on Western civilization?

James is seeking to explain the meaning of socialism. For him, socialism is complete democracy. Therefore, he begins the first lecture with democracy in the ancient Greek City-State. He tells us why: "because I could not do without it." The Greeks invented direct democracy.[3]

From Greece he goes to Rome and the Revelations of St. John. He says he chose John because he was a colonial subject of Rome. John had a sense of historic sweep, and in his vision of God's Kingdom he was addressing the questions that occupied the Greeks, above all the relation of the individual and the collective.

From the ancient world James moves to the City-States of the Middle Ages and to the class struggles that tore them apart. He talks about the English Civil War and the birth of a new form of government, represent-

---

1   I am grateful to Geert Dhondt and John Garvey for their suggestions.
2   A fuller outline of James's life and thought can be found in my introduction to *A New Notion* (PM Press, 2010).
3   James explores this subject at greater length in "Every Cook Can Govern," reprinted in *A New Notion: Two Works by C.L.R. James* (Oakland: PM Press, 2010).

ative democracy,[4] citing Shakespeare, "the great dramatist of individual character," as an example of the emerging spirit. (James referred to Shakespeare frequently in his works; a series of lectures on Shakespeare he delivered on the BBC has been lost.) He takes up philosophy and the Age of Reason, and Rousseau's repudiation of that way of thinking and of representative government. After touching on the American and French Revolutions, he ends the lecture by defining the problem he will be addressing: "Much of our study of modern politics is going to be concerned with this tremendous battle to find a form of government which reproduces, on a more highly developed economic level, the relationship between the individual and the community that was established so wonderfully in the Greek City-State."

The classics of the West have shaped the modern world. The European Renaissance was a moment of world-historic significance, and the great works of antiquity were sources of it. However, to accept a genealogy in which "ancient Greece begat Rome, Rome begat Christian Europe, Christian Europe begat the Renaissance, the Renaissance the Enlightenment, the Enlightenment political democracy and the industrial revolution" and so forth is misleading.[5]

The ancient Greeks traced their culture back to Egypt.[6] Egypt drew upon the Upper Nile (modern Sudan). The Book of Genesis came from Mesopotamia; according to the Biblical account, Abraham was an Iraqi shepherd. During the Hellenistic age, Greece faced east, not west; Alexander the Great conquered Persia, and Persia conquered Alexander. Christian doctrine drew heavily on notions that were circulating widely in the Eastern Mediterranean, including matings between gods and humans, virgin birth, the Messiah, resurrection and afterlife.[7]

---

4    Ellen Meiksins Wood traces the devolution from direct to representative democracy in *Democracy Against Capitalism: Renewing Historical Materialism* (Cambridge: Cambridge University Press, 1995). She makes no reference to James.
5    Eric Wolf, *Europe and the People Without History* (Berkeley: University of California Press, 1982) 5.
6    See Martin Bernal, *Black Athena: The Afroasiatic Roots of Classical Civilization* (New Brunswick, NJ: Rutgers University Press, 1987).
7    For more on this, see Archibald Robertson, *The Origins of Christianity* (New York: International Publishers, 1954), and the classic *Foundations of Christianity: A Study in Christian Origins* by Karl Kautsky (New York: Monthly Review, 1972).

Following the "fall" of Rome, Byzantium and the Islamic world preserved the works of the Greeks and Romans and kept alive the classical traditions of humanism and scientific inquiry. Islam was influenced by East and West.

Cultures are not products of regions isolated from each other.

Settled agriculture, urban life, patriarchal religion and the state were born in the Tigris-Euphrates Valley around 7000 BCE. The first literary object to emerge from Britain that anyone from anywhere else would take any interest in was Beowulf, c. 1000 CE. In other words, about eight thousand years elapsed between the birth of what is called civilization and anything of literary value from Britain, three thousand miles away. Yet that vast gap in time and space did not prevent the inhabitants of Britain from going on to lead the world in producing works from Chaucer to Jane Austen and beyond that illuminated the human condition everywhere, nor has it stopped them from asserting their ownership of literary works they had no direct hand in producing.

And that is as it should be. Everything created by human beings anywhere is and ought to be the property of all human beings everywhere. I used to know a poet who called Milton black. On being asked why, she replied, "Well, I'm black and I like him."

C.L.R. James would have agreed with her. (He refers to *Paradise Lost* in these lectures, comparing it to the Revelations of St. John.)

•

Class struggle is a constant theme in the lectures. Whether talking about fifteenth-century Flemish City-States or twentieth-century Detroit, James stresses the class struggle as the force that drives history. When I met James, he asked me what I did for a living. I told him I worked in a factory. He said he regretted that he never had the opportunity to do that. I naturally replied that his writings had helped me make sense of my own experience. Yes, he said, people have told me that, but I still wish I had experienced it directly. In order to illustrate James's world view and as partial repayment for what he taught me, I shall here recount some things I saw in twenty-three years as a worker in industry.

I once had a job operating a horizontal boring mill in a plant that manufactured punch presses, machine tools and die sets. My job was to bore holes and mill contours on large—often 6' × 8"—steel slabs to be made into die sets to customers' specifications. The mill was an old-fashioned, manually controlled machine, well built and originally quite expensive, capable of turning out high-quality work.

The plant operated on an incentive-pay system: each job was time-rated for the machine on which it was to be performed, and the operator received a bonus for all he or she managed to produce above the eight-hour norm. Jobs varied, but the bonus could account for as much a half a worker's total wage.

In order to be fair to the employees on the bonus system—and the company was nothing if not fair—it was necessary to make allowance for the time spent outside of direct production, sharpening tools, loading parts on the machine (including waiting for the overhead crane when it was occupied elsewhere), filling the coolant tank and so forth. The allowances were recorded through red computer-coded cards punched in a clock.

When I started on the job, one of the veteran operators called me aside and explained the system. "You see those red cards?" he asked, pointing at the rack where they were stacked. "If the company won't give you a raise, you take those red cards and give yourself a raise. That's what they're for."

I took his advice and studied hard and soon became sufficiently adept with the red cards to assure myself several hours' bonus most days. I remember one of the operators asking me what I considered the most valuable tool in my box. I held up a pencil.

To lower costs, the company installed a new tape-controlled mill, able to do more or less the same work as the one I was on in about half the time. They then reset the standards, reducing the time allotted for all jobs, even those still being sent to the old machine. Our bonuses evaporated.

There were three of us on the horizontal mill, one on each shift. We petitioned for a return to the old rates. The company denied our petition. With the new rates, the most we could turn out, even with intense effort and trouble-free operation, was six hours' production. Why should we strain ourselves to make the same hourly rate we could make by coasting? We slowed down.

As I recall, our slowdown was undertaken without a single meeting among the three of us. (Our different shifts meant we were never all together, although each of us saw the other two every day.) One of us—I no longer remember who—simply announced one day to the operator coming after him, "I'm fed up with this. I gave them an hour and a half tonight and that's all I'm doing from now on." The next operator followed his lead, and it became standard practice on reporting for work to inquire of the departing operator how much he had turned out and to do the same or less. After a few weeks we had established our own norm, around three quarters of an hour each shift.

Of course the company did not like what was going on, but without assigning a foreman to observe each of us full-time, how were they to know when a tool burned up and needed replacing, or how long the operator needed to wait for a new one to be ground when the tool crib was out of the required tool, or when the coolant in the machine needed replenishing, or when the crane was occupied or out of order, or the crane operator was on break—or any of the mysteries of a horizontal boring mill operator's life, each faithfully recorded on a red card and entered into the computer that never lies?

Things went along for a while with us pretending to work and the company pretending to pay us, until one day the general foreman announced that since production on the horizontal mill was so low the company was eliminating one of the three operators. Since I was the newest, the ax would fall on me. I was offered a choice between taking a layoff or retraining on the tape-controlled machine. I chose the latter and was soon third-shift operator. The other two horizontal mill operators continued their slowdown without me. Shortly afterward, the company transferred them to another department and sold the machine to a salvage company for a fraction of its cost.

The episode was a small example of Marx's observation that the class struggle led either to a revolutionary reconstitution of the society or the common ruin of the contending classes. The three of us had destroyed that horizontal mill just as effectively as if we had taken a torch and sledgehammer to it. Although it remained physically intact and capable of performing the tasks for which it had been designed and built, it no longer existed as capital, the only form of value in a capitalist society.

•

The Tractor Works of the International Harvester Company was located across the street from the McCormick Reaper Works, the original plant of the Harvester Company and scene of the eight-hour-day strike of 1886 that led to the May First holiday. In 1940, when the CIO finally forced Harvester to recognize it as the bargaining agent, Lucy Parsons—labor organizer and widow of Albert Parsons, martyred in 1886—declared to assembled workers, "Now I know my husband didn't die in vain."

One of the products of the plant was earth-moving tractors. (Although foremen insisted that the proper term for that type of tractor was the generic "crawler," the workers perversely referred to them as "Caterpillars.") One of the customers was the government, which used them to fill bomb craters in Vietnam. The standard joke was that the soldiers drove them into the craters and shoveled dirt on top of them.

By 1968 the inmates were running the asylum. Wishing to recover the ability to plan production, Harvester launched a campaign against absenteeism, beginning by seeking to fire the worst offenders. They called in the chairman of the union grievance committee and showed him the record of one especially flagrant case showing seventeen dates over the span of a year.

"Why you bastards," yelled the committeeman, "you want to fire this guy and he's only missed seventeen days, and you don't even know what kind of problems he's been having . . ." and so on.

"Hold on, Bill," replied the personnel director. "These aren't the days he missed. These are the days he came to work last year."

What everyone in the plant knew, which never came out in the hearing, was that the guy had started up an ice cream parlor on the outside and was spending all his time there, hanging onto his job at Harvester for the health insurance. The most Harvester could get was a thirty-day suspension—like throwing Br'er Rabbit in the briar patch.

•

When I started in the steel mills, I was astonished at the extent to which the workers there had established control over the workday. In part, the power of the workers was a consequence of the way steel was produced: once the iron ore, coke and limestone are in the furnace, they can't be drilled, or assembled, or stacked up, or any of the other things done on assembly lines. The technique is not the whole story, however, because the steel companies were always trying to combine jobs to make people work during the slack time dictated by the furnaces. The workers resisted them at every turn: In 1959 there was a three-month strike over job descriptions, one manifestation of the ongoing war. At Harvester's subsidiary, Wisconsin Steel, the management tried for several years to change the system whereby workers picked up their time cards at the mill entrance and handed them in to the foremen in their work areas to one in which they punched in at the entrance. The workers responded with several strikes, which appeared a mystery—why should people care where they hand in their cards? Talking to the workers revealed that many of them had private arrangements with their foremen, which allowed them to hand in their cards and then disappear for the rest of their shift. Having to hand in their time cards at the entrance to plant guards they did not know would have interfered with these arrangements.

I remember at U.S. Steel a foreman once came into a shanty where a bunch of maintenance workers were sitting around, some drinking coffee, some playing cards, some snoozing, and asked two of them to go out and see about a certain piece of equipment that was broken.

"Can't you see I'm busy?" said one of them as he picked up the cards for the next deal.

"We'll get it when the rain stops," said another.

The foreman exited, apparently satisfied that he had got the most he could from that group at that moment. Of course that situation prevailed among maintenance more than production workers, and the line between them partly corresponded to the color line—but not entirely. I once asked a fellow worker, a black woman, why there were so few wildcat strikes in the steel mill compared to a nearby auto plant well known for their frequency. Without hesitating, she said, "It's because people here are always on strike."[8]

Her answer stood out against the attitude of one of the more prominent left-wing trade unionists in the Calumet area, whom I visited shortly after I began work in the mill. I asked him about the movement of workers in the industry.

"What movement?" he replied. "There is no movement."

---

8    She made another comment I wish to record: "I've been in prison, I've been in a mental hospital, and I've been at U.S. Steel. As far as I'm concerned, this is the strangest of them all: in those other places people knew something was wrong, and around here people think that what they do is normal."

I knew that in his mill the workers in some departments were making their rates in half a shift and spending the other half in the tavern nearby. I asked him about it. "That's not a movement," he said. "They've been doing that for years. It doesn't mean anything."

To him, "movement" meant the number of workers who attended union meetings, voted for the resolutions introduced by his caucus and supported his slate at election time. The accumulation of shop-floor battles that had ripped half the day out of the hands of capital was not part of the class struggle as it existed in his mind.

C.L.R. James taught otherwise. So did Marx, who devoted a chapter in *Capital* to the struggle over the length of the working day. Of all the dogmas that hold sway among leftists, the most widespread and pernicious is the dogma of the backwardness of the working class. To adhere to it is to reject Marxism root and branch, for Marxism holds that the capitalist system revolutionizes the forces of production and that the working class is foremost among the forces of production.

•

A black woman I worked with told me that when she first started in a new position at the plant as a crane operator she got no help from the others in the department, all white men. Contrary to their usual practice, whenever she was on the crane they would hook up the loads so that they were hard to move, and in general did what they could to make her job more difficult than necessary. After a few weeks she called them all together and delivered a speech: "Listen, you motherfuckers, I'm not asking for special consideration as a woman. I just want to be respected as a crane operator. I've got rent to pay and babies to feed just like you, so I don't care what you do, you're not running me out of here."

They changed their attitudes and became totally cooperative. Let no one think the victory was hers alone: she was a harbinger of the new society, a "fully developed individual, fit for a variety of labors, ready to face any change of production, to whom the different social functions [s]he performs are but so many modes of giving free scope to [her] own natural and acquired powers" (from *Capital*, Volume I, Chapter 15, the only passage from Marx that James quoted in these six lectures).

James's revolutionary optimism was inspired and sustained by his deep appreciation for the kinds of experiences I have recounted. Those experiences were hallmarks of the period when large numbers of workers were brought together in factories and where they had the opportunity, and took it, to impose some control over their work circumstances, taking advantage of the cover provided by a union and contract. Today, in the United States, the ability of workers to assert that kind of control in a single workplace is diminished. The situation may be different in India and China.

•

If James teaches us anything, he teaches us to look. I knew a radical in 1969 who took a job as a truck driver and after a few weeks reported that the chances of collective action among truck drivers was slim since their work dictated that they be isolated as individuals instead of being brought together in large concentrations. Then someone invented the CB radio, and the result was a national wildcat strike of owner-operators. In part out of fear of working class strength, capital broke up or greatly reduced in size the large centers of proletarian concentration, the River Rouges, the Gary Works, the FIAT Mirafiori works. Yet in pursuit of its own need to coordinate production (including research) and distribution on a world scale, capital gave us the internet, with the result that a man who sets himself on fire in Tunisia in protest against high prices touches off a wave of struggle that topples a government in Egypt, which in turn serves as an example to people in Madison, Wisconsin, which inspires the Occupy movement (which seems to have gone into fatal decline, to be surely followed by new struggles).

James has been criticized for failing to acknowledge or explain defeats in the class struggle. Like any person engaged in serious day-to-day politics, he found it necessary to take into account and adapt to setbacks.[9] But his overall outlook led him to seek out the future in the present. In this respect he brings to mind the Abolitionist Wendell Phillips, who declared in a speech following John Brown's raid on Harpers Ferry, "What is defeat? Nothing but education—nothing but

---

9    In a little-known address he delivered in London in 1967 on the death of Che Guevara, James predicted that if the capitalist system continued on the path of destroying the material elements of civilization, rendering impossible traditional means of struggle, then guerrilla warfare could become the only method open.

the first step to something better"—and was proven right within a few years.

•

It was James's custom to speak without notes, and there is every reason to believe that he delivered these lectures that way (although they may have been edited later for publication). He was able to do so because he had thoroughly mastered his subject matter. Like a great athlete who pulls off amazing feats on the court, his mastery was due to the countless hours he put in off the court or the lectern. In *Modern Politics* James stresses that philosophy must become proletarian, which is to be understood to mean that philosophers must embrace the proletariat and the proletariat must embrace philosophy. Whatever our disappointments and difficulties at the moment, his wisdom needs to be reaffirmed. Not long ago I took part in a two-person panel at a conference of mostly young activists. The panel was set up as a debate, and each of us circulated well in advance a five-page essay we believed would help the discussion. When my turn came to speak, I asked that those who had not read the essays refrain from speaking in the discussion that would follow our opening remarks. I do not know how many of those who spoke had read the material we circulated, and I had no way of enforcing my request. Afterwards, one person, who had not spoken, came up to me and said she was offended, saying she felt "disempowered" by my request that she not take part. I replied that I had not asked her not to take part, merely not to speak, and that she was welcome to listen. My reply made no difference. I later learned that others shared her feelings. I asked myself, what would C.L.R. James (or Malcolm X) have said?

•

James devotes part of the final lecture to what he calls "the undying vision," a survey of works of art he believes point the way toward the future. He names D.W. Griffith, Chaplin and Picasso. All of them, he argues, were shaped by the need to serve a popular audience. Elsewhere he had said the same about the Greeks and Shakespeare. One of my teachers in high school, Dr. Gordon, told us that if we had gone up to someone on the street in London in 1605 and asked the names of the best poets, the answer would have been Marlowe or Donne or Jonson. If we had asked about Shakespeare, our informant would have slapped his upper leg and said, Will Shakespeare—why, he's the best playwright in town! Theater was seen as popular entertainment, not serious literature. Dr. Gordon would have shared James's view. If Shakespeare were alive today, he would be writing for the movies.

•

James concludes, "Anyone who tries to prevent you from knowing, from learning anything, is an enemy, an enemy of freedom, of equality, of democracy." His words were prophetic: scarcely were the lectures published in book form when Prime Minister Williams ordered the books suppressed, placing them under guard in a warehouse in Port of Spain. In his Introduction to the 1973 edition of *Modern Politics* (included in this volume), Martin Glaberman provides the context; I won't repeat what he wrote. James left Trinidad. Later, when he reentered the country, Williams placed him under house arrest. Thus James joined the long and honorable list of those who were locked up for what they wrote.

•

One turns to C.L.R. James for many reasons. If pressed I would say *Mariners, Renegades and Castaways: The Story of Herman Melville and the World We Live In* is my favorite among his works. Yet for comprehensiveness, integration of history, philosophy, culture, politics and method, as an introduction to Marxism and socialism for new readers, *Modern Politics* is in first place. John Bracey, who was part of the group that brought James back to the States in 1967, tells of the time James called his attention to a football game on television: "Look at that, Bracey," he said, "black people beating up white people on TV—capitalism is doomed." It is hard to imagine an anecdote that captures and brings together so many different facets of C.L.R. James. *Modern Politics* is that story elaborated over six lectures.

# Introduction

WHEN THE LECTURES which make up this book were delivered, C.L.R. James was the editor of *The Nation*, the organ of the People's National Movement. The leader of PNM was Eric Williams, a student and old friend of James, who had come back to Trinidad to found the party that was to lead Trinidad to national independence. However, at what seemed to be the moment of victory, a split developed between Williams and James over the nature and future of independence. Williams began a massive retreat from the objectives of the PNM, especially in relation to concessions to American imperialism. The retreat was embodied in the dispute over the Chaguaramas Naval Base, a piece of Trinidad territory which the British, with their usual generosity, had given to the United States on a long-term lease. A major demand of the independence movement had been the return of Chaguaramas to the people of Trinidad. When Eric Williams abandoned that demand it was a sign that his struggle against colonialism would not go beyond the acceptance of neo-colonialism and the trading of British for American imperialism. That was a direction which James refused to go and the break between the two old friends very quickly became complete.

In his preface to the printed edition of his lectures, James hinted at the seriousness of the dispute and the dangers involved. He wrote that "whoever, for whatever reason, puts barriers in the way of knowledge is thereby automatically convicted of reaction and enmity to human progress." As if to confirm his fears, Williams ordered the suppression of this book and for many years the printed volumes lay in a warehouse in Port of Spain under guard. Ultimately, Williams relented to the extent of letting a New York book dealer buy the lot and take it out of the country. That limited edition, long suppressed and then, briefly, available, is now being reprinted.

The interest in this book extends far beyond the West Indies. In explaining the meaning of socialism to an audience in an underdeveloped country, James has made the struggle for socialism universal. It is a book that I believe will in time become known throughout the world, a book that will make the meaning of socialism clear to millions.

Martin Glaberman
September 15, 1973

# Preface

I WANT TO say here the great gratitude and personal satisfaction that I feel, first at having had the opportunity to give these lectures and secondly to know that they have been printed for public circulation. If at the end of my three-year stay in the West Indies this was all that I had to show, I would be amply satisfied.

First: we shall soon have at the United Nations a representative who will take part in the great debate (which is now shaking the world in theory and tomorrow may shake it in arms) as to the validity of the ideas which I have put forward here and their embodiment in life. The public cannot know too much of the premises on which these great decisions, in politics and elsewhere, are being and will be made.

Secondly: it is and has been for years my unshakable conviction that sooner or later the people of the West Indies, as people everywhere else, will be faced with practical choices and decisions on their attitude to Marxism. Marxism, as I have tried to show, covers a wide variety of theory and practice. It is my hope that these lectures will contribute to a wise choice, if and when the choice has to be made, to whatever extent and degree. A mistake could ruin our lives for at least a generation.

In the end it is practical life and its needs which will decide both the problems of social and political existence and the correctness of a theory. But mankind has today reached a stage where action is conditioned by thought and thought by action to a degree unprecedented in previous ages. That indeed is the problem of our twentieth century. Whatever helps to clarify this is valuable. And whoever, for whatever reason, puts barriers in the way of knowledge is thereby automatically convicted of reaction and enmity to human progress.

C.L.R. James

# Chapter One
## Monday, 8th August, 1960

MR. CHAIRMAN, LADIES AND GENTLEMEN:

I am about to speak on a subject which is as difficult as it is possible to be, particularly to be treated in a series of public lectures. Nevertheless, when the subject was first broached to me, I welcomed it, because whatever the difficulties—and those you will share with me, to some degree—the West Indies are, in the near future, going to enter into the great big world outside as an independent force. Despite the difficulties in the way, I think we should not miss any opportunity to investigate, from every possible point of view, the realities and probabilities of the world of which we shall soon be a constituent part. It is with that in view that I shall speak this evening and in the rest of the lectures.

I will not disguise from you that I have a particular point of view. I am a Marxist. However, my Marxism—there are always different styles of any particular doctrine that is so widespread as Marxism is—my Marxism has little connection with the Marxism that people in Communist China and Communist Russia and various other territories profess. That you will see as I develop my ideas. But I want to make something quite clear: I am not here in order to propagandize you, that is to say, to make you accept or believe certain ideas. I am not here to agitate you, that is to say, to get you to take certain actions. I am speaking here from the point of view of exposition; I am explaining a point of view. It is inevitable, where serious matters as these are concerned, that I shall speak about people and things to whom I am opposed, if not with too much energy—I shall try to restrain that—but certainly with a certain amount of scorn and contempt which they, in their turn, in my position, would not hesitate to apply to me. (laughter) But inasmuch as this is a series of lectures—and it is knowledge rather than action which guides this forum here—I propose as far as possible (and some of the points on which I shall take a position are very difficult indeed, and I am aware of the strength of the opposing arguments), I shall try for the sake of a rounded position to let you know what are the solid arguments against the views that I am putting forward.

I do not propose to be impartial. Any public lecturer on politics who says he is impartial is either an idiot or a traitor. You cannot be impartial in matters of this kind; but you can present a rounded point of view, and at question time and discussion time, I will be quite willing, not only willing, but will welcome any fairly consistent point of view which is opposed to the point of view I hold.

You will have noticed that I have got five points, more or less, in every lecture. Now every lecture is to last for about seventy-five minutes, not more, and I hope less. Five points mean at best fifteen minutes on each, fifteen minutes or a little less, because there must be a little introduction, and there must be, perhaps, a little conclusion. So when I say Point No. 1, Plato, Aristotle and the Greek City-State, it is clear that I intend no elaborate analysis either of the facts or any ideas which we can draw from them. I want to make that clear. I select the Greek City-State because I could not do without it; and I take Plato and Aristotle to make one or two references to establish certain fundamental premises; and from these premises I will draw as time goes on. But I mention these first because I say they are necessary; and secondly because after all what we are aiming at here is the expansion of ideas and the development of interest; and this will guide you to some of the things that I am saying and enable you, if you are students, either to refresh your memory, or if you are just beginning, to follow up when you leave here.

## What We Owe to Ancient Greece

Now I begin with the Greek City-States. The Greek City-States were a group of states centered around the Aegean Sea and the Mediterranean; they had some colonies further out, but those are not so important. The largest of them was certainly Athens; and the number of citizens in Athens was perhaps forty or fifty thousand. They had a number of slaves, but the legitimate citizens might be about forty or fifty thousand people. They were also quite poor; the land was not good. In an island like Barbados, I believe there is more wealth and material goods accumulated today than existed in all the Greek City-States added together. Yet these states, with Athens at the head, formed, in my opinion, the most remarkable of all the various civilizations of which we have record in history, including our own. In politics, in ethics, in science, in philosophy, in epic poetry, in tragic drama, in comic drama, in sculpture, in medicine, in science, they laid the foundations of Western civilization. And it is not only that we today rest upon their achievements. It is far more wonderful than that. If today you want to study politics, it is not because Aristotle and Plato began the great discussion, not at all; in order to tackle politics today, fundamentally, you have to read them for the questions that they pose and the way that they pose them; they are not superseded at all.

Now what were the reasons for the strength of this remarkable exhibition of civic, social and political organization? These questions are still disputed. I can select only two. They are, for me, the most important, and also they are the most important for this series of lectures. The first is that in the great days of the City-State of Athens in particular, the Athenians rejected representative government and followed a pattern of direct democracy.

I am going to make this as vivid as possible.

## How Direct Democracy Worked

Athens was divided into ten tribes or divisions, and every month they selected by lot a certain number of men from each division. (You put names in a hat and pull them out. I don't know the particular method by which they chose.) And these went into the government offices and governed the state for that month. They required two things of him: (1) that he had fought in the wars; and (2) that he had paid his taxes; also, I think, that his family, his old parents were properly seen after. They did not ask whether you could read or you could write. I would suspect that a great number of them were illiterate. At the end of that period they went out and another set came in, chosen in the same way. It wasn't that they didn't know about representative government; they had had representative government and they rejected it in favor of this system of direct democracy. Now if you went—I will not be local—but if you went to some foreign country and told the leaders there, the mayor and councilors, that their city could be governed by just taking any thirty people, by putting names in a hat and choosing these, our modern rulers would fall apart. They would consider that that was absolutely impossible, if they were not students; if they were, they would be a little bit more careful because they would have the Greeks in their minds; and I believe they would be quite right. I doubt if you could take thirty or forty people today from anywhere and put them into some government, however small it might be, and ask them to run it. It is not because government is so difficult. The idea that a little municipality, as we have them all over the world today, would have more difficult and complex problems than the city of Athens is quite absurd. *It is that people have lost the habit of looking at government and one another in that way.* It isn't in their minds at all. To the Greeks, after centuries of experiment with political methods, it was a natural procedure; it lasted for two hundred years, and that was the government which produced what we live on intellectually to this day.

## The Relation of the Greek to His Government

The second point that I wish to make flows from that one, and it is this: In my opinion the greatest strength of the Greek government, the Greek ancient democracy, was that it achieved a balance between the individual and the community that was never achieved before or since. That is one of the fundamental problems of politics: what is the relation of the individual, his rights, his liberties, his freedom, his possibilities of progress to the community in which he lives as a part? And nowhere, as far as I know, was this so finely achieved, this balance so beautifully managed, as between the individual citizen and the City-State of ancient Greece.

Now, I mention Plato and Aristotle. They both detested the City-State. They were very learned men, and naturally they disapproved of government by all sorts of persons picked up by chance. Nevertheless, when Plato had the opportunity to live in Athens, when the reaction had established a dictatorship, he had the grace to say that, after all, he didn't like any of them, but the democracy was better than a dictatorship. And Aristotle said that there were governments of democracy and of oligarchy and aristocracy—and none of them was very good, was absolutely perfect—but on the whole the least bad of them was a bad democracy, and, therefore, he gave his support also to this extreme democracy.

Plato and Aristotle, however, owe their great reputations to the penetration that they showed in analyzing the problems of government. I will have to leave to you to work out the particular aspects you wish to tackle. But today it is recognized that if they were able to penetrate so deeply into fundamental problems and to write so freely and develop their ideas, it was not due only to their extraordinary ability. (Aristotle is perhaps one of the three ablest men I have any knowledge of.) It was because of the state which they analyzed, and in all their analyses they were constantly seeking how to improve the City-State; and the penetration of their work, its range, its vitality, up to today, is due to the fact that the state that they lived in and that they examined was of this remarkable character. It was not perfect, but it was of such a type that it posed all the fundamental questions, and so solved them that it enabled these philosophers to write as they have written.

The next section that I propose to deal with this evening is Rome, and I have put next to Rome, St. John of Revelations. The devil can quote Scripture for his purpose but Scripture is Scripture, and I am prepared to use it. (laughter)

## Great Rome and Little Athens

Rome is important for us for various reasons; one of them is the contrast with Athens. Athens at its best was small—you go down to the Oval and you watch cricket down there, about thirty thousand people—that was about the number of citizens in Athens in its best days. The Romans were different. That was the greatest empire the world has ever seen without a doubt, because it occupied the whole of the known world. Whatever the Romans didn't rule was barbarism—remote places; nobody could get there. They certainly have left a great influence in various parts of Europe, but, nevertheless, on the whole, their influence in the world is much less than that of little scrappy Athens. They left a great heritage of law. In any case the point I wish to make is that it is not size, it is not strength, it is not power; it is what you do with what you have that matters. And Greece showed that you can have very little and still achieve the things which stand out as among the greatest achievements of humanity. (applause)

Rome fell, collapsed, became a laughing stock among all the backward barbarians whom it had ruled. And I take St. John of Revelations for one reason: he was a colonial. He was a Jew whose country was ruled by the Romans; and he was anti-imperialist and anti-colonialist. If you want to read about anti-imperialism and anti-colonialism, take the Bible and read the last Book, that is the *Revelations of St. John.* John called them such a set of fornicators, whoremongers, Sodomites, corruptors—every conceivable piece of abuse that you could find—you will see there what he said about those Romans. He didn't like them. If he wrote like that today in any ordinary colony they would arrest him, not, perhaps, for sedition, but certainly for—what is the phrase?—disrespect or something? Violent and obscene language.

## St. John's Vision of a Harmonious Society

He says that Rome is to be destroyed; and he means destroyed. He is not speaking metaphorically. He said that the Heavens are going to open and that Christ is going to come with mighty armies; and he even chose the place of the battle, Armageddon. There the great battle is going to be fought; and the Romans are going to be beaten, defeated, ruined, and there is going to be such a slaughter that before the armies of Christ come down, somebody is going to come out and call all the birds of the air, the vultures, *corbeaux*, and the rest of them, so that when the battle is over they can eat up all the dead bodies.

He says Babylon is fallen—that great city. He had some respect for his own hide. He wouldn't write Rome; he said it was Babylon, but everybody knew whom he meant.

What is important for us, however, is that two aspects of political life at critical moments appear in his work. Number one: he had a historical sweep. He said that there had been four monarchies. I cannot remember exactly. I think one was the Macedonians, another was the Egyptians, another one was the Assyrians and so forth. But he said the Romans were the last; and then would come the Kingdom of God on earth. You see, he had a sense of historical development. His was the fifth monarchy. There had been four monarchies, and the fifth monarchy would be the Kingdom of God on earth.

And then he said something else. In his own way he was concerned with the same problems that Plato and Aristotle and all the serious thinkers were concerned with. He said there would be a new world after the Romans had been defeated, and everybody would be happy. He said there would be no sea. In other words, the problem of crossing the sea was giving that generation a lot of trouble, so the new world would have no sea—God would see about that—so you could move about as you please. He says, again, the fruits of the earth would bear every month; it is those that we have which bear every twelve months; his was to be every month. There would always be plenty to eat. And he says that the lion and the lamb would lie down in peace.

If I have said a few things about him which would give you an idea that he was not a very great writer, it is because I am trying to point out certain aspects of his works. I personally have, over the years, found that, as a religious poem—because that is what it is, though it was based on fact—it can stand comparison with Milton's *Paradise Lost*, and, by and large, if I had to choose one—which Heaven forbid I will ever have to do—I think I would take St. John; and not because he is anti-imperialist, but because of the strength of his vision, his grasp of fundamentals, and his kinship, despite the peculiar form that he used, with great philosophers like Plato and Aristotle. He was dominated by the vision of a peaceful and harmonious society.

## The City-States of the Middle Ages

The next group I have chosen is the City-States of the Middle Ages, particularly in Italy and Flanders. Now again we have the extraordinary spectacle of City-States—Genoa, Florence, Siena, Pisa, Padua, Rome; a number of them in Spain; but the ones I want to speak about particularly are in Flanders: Ghent, Bruges, Antwerp, and various others of the kind—City-States.

They were of a type different from the City-States of Greece, whence their troubles began, but whence, also, arose their glory—those in Ghent and in Flanders. Those in northern Italy, particularly Florence, practiced a type of capitalism; that is to say, they assembled workers (who had neither property nor land) in factories, and with a co-operative type of labor, produced goods, for the most part textiles. The wealth that they produced, particularly in comparison with the standards of wealth of the countries around them, was beyond belief. The moment you have this collection of men doing co-operative labor according to a fixed plan—which is essentially what capitalism is; a fixed plan inside the factory, at any rate—there you have possibilities of wealth that no previous type of economy was ever able to manage. Whereas the City-States of Greece were extremely poor in material wealth, the City States of the Middle Ages were extremely wealthy, particularly those in northern Italy and in Flanders. Antwerp was the port of the City-States of Flanders, and they say five hundred ships came in there every day; and however small they were, five hundred ships every day is a great number of ships indeed! The rulers in Ghent and in particular in Bruges were men so wealthy—the mayors of those cities—that they sent embassies to kings, received embassies; had fleets and armies of their own, and treated with the rulers of France and England and the rest on equal terms, although they lived and ruled only in a single city.

Their achievements were magnificent. Just as an example. In Florence, somewhere in the sixteenth century, when the municipality wanted to have a competition as to who should paint panels in the City Hall, the winners of the competition were two Florentine citizens— Michelangelo and Leonardo da Vinci. That was greatness indeed.

At the same time in Florence there was Donatello, perhaps one of the greatest sculptors after Michelangelo. In the great cathedral there, Dante, the greatest of European writers, used to be sitting down, watching his friend, Giotto, the great painter, build the tremendous tower which is next to the cathedral; and walking on the banks of the Arno would be Dante's friend, Guido Cavalcanti. Dante is the great Catholic poet, but when Guido was walking all by himself there, with his face deep in thought, people used to say, "Look at him. He is there looking for arguments to prove that there is no God." But Dante was his good friend.

Two of the greatest painters that the world has ever known, the Van Eycks—they came to fruition in Flanders with many others around them. You go to Flanders and see those town halls and other buildings— magnificent up to this day. But they collapsed like Rome. And the reason why they collapsed, is of great importance to us. Employers and workers for centuries fought some of the bitterest struggles that you can think of in all the history of the labor movement. You see, the moment they got the workers together in one factory, and you had eight or ten factories, and they were all in one city, then that was trouble! In the last half of the fifteenth century, we have fifty years of continuous battles, and of attempts by the workers in those cities five hundred years ago to establish what we can legitimately call Workers' States. In a few places they did manage it. Sometimes only for a few weeks, sometimes for a few months, once for three or four years. The persistence and energy of those attempts is incredible. One of the names you might remember is Van Artevelde, a member of a family that took a great part in this business. At one time they had the idea of establishing a workers' government right through Flanders, Holland and Belgium, and had all the ruling groups and kings and the rest of them in Western Europe shivering in their shoes. They were beaten in the end—the clergy, the aristocracy, the bourgeoisie, the artisans, not the wage laborers, you see, but the independent artisans, all joined together and with some knights in armor defeated them in a battle. That is how they were beaten.

I want to give you a certain episode and I want you to reflect on it, because it is very important in approaching history and political matters. At a certain stage under the leadership of Van Artevelde, who, by the way, was a bourgeois, but he joined the working class movement—they decided that the only thing that they could do to have peace in the city was to wipe away the employing class completely—men, women and children, everybody over the age of six. (laughter)

Now I bring that to your notice and I would like you to reflect on it, because here is the central question of political theory and political philosophy. It is not only an unusual, but it is an extreme state of mind when, not one or two people, but a whole population—members of a class living a certain life—reach the stage of exasperation when they feel that they will have to rid themselves of a whole class. They must be no more than six years of age; if they are at all older than that, they grow up and give a lot of trouble. You see, they feel this stage of exasperation with something that has been going on for many years. But the employers also (you have got to look at their point of view—after all you can afford to be judicious, because this took place many hundred years ago), the employers also are obviously in face of what is for them an insoluble difficulty. It is a problem that cannot be solved, and was not solved. You know what happened? Those City-States collapsed from the violence of the internal struggles, which means that it is not evil, and malice, and cruelty that comes into play. It is an objective social and political situation that is beyond the solution of those who are taking part and they slash and fight and cut up one another until, finally, those states collapsed. For us, in this forum, it is important to remember what they were seeking—the weavers and these others in particular. They were seeking to establish what Plato and Aristotle had written about, and what St. John had in mind after the Roman Empire was overthrown. They were seeking to establish some sort of government in which there would be no extra privileges or extra authority except for those who actually labored. They failed, the regime collapsed and the national State superseded them. But we are at an important part of the study of politics, to see to what extent an insoluble problem can tear to pieces and ruin those persons who are engaged in it.

*You of course understand that we are engaged in much the same type of problem today.*

I do not say it is insoluble, but it is good to have some sort of balance and to recognize the objective nature of problems and what they do to people; and it is not the evil in people that creates problems but the problems that create the evil. In the course of a political struggle you throw bricks and call your opponent enemy and scoundrel and thief and rogue, but that cannot be helped because he is doing the same thing. But if you are studying politics seriously you have to see where the objective problems lie and what are the possibilities of solution. That is what I mean by some problems of method.

## The Birth of Parliamentary Democracy

We now come to the modern world, we are a little closer—the seventeenth century—Great Britain. And we come to the establishment of the principles of parliamentary democracy. And these did not come from people who had studied Plato and Aristotle, nor by people who studied St. John, although St. John comes in a little later. The principles of democracy came in a way that is very instructive to us because my experience, limited as it has been, shows that, by and large, the great political discoveries, although heralded by great writers and in the speeches of politicians, the great political discoveries, the actual discoveries of actual policy, come as much by the instinctive actions of masses of people as by anything else. No scholars or philosophers work them out.

I will have to be very brief, very concise. I shall do a lot of injustice to some very excellent people and to some execrable people, but it cannot be helped. In England in the seventeenth century, you have a corrupt monarchy—corrupt in the sense that it was no longer suitable for the work that it had to do. You had a feudal aristocracy surrounding the monarchy, and that was Anglo-Catholic. They had broken away from the Roman Catholic Church but they still retained many of the practices and attitudes of the Roman Church. They were Episcopalian, but the King could marry Henrietta of France, who was a Catholic.

Opposed to the King were the gentry. They owned land on the countryside, but they were progressive farmers. And also opposed to the King more or less were the merchants in the towns.

Now the frame of society in those days, the external and to some degree the internal frame, was religious, and these struggles were fought out over political and economic problems but, fundamentally, in a religious ideology and in religious terms. The King and those around him were Protestants, high church Episcopalians. The gentry, the progressive farmers, (and some of them were noblemen, by the way) and the merchants were Presbyterians. They were actually called that—the Presbyterian Party.

## Cromwell and the Levellers

Now for thirty or forty years—longer perhaps—the Presbyterians carried on a steady attack against the Episcopalian Church through which the King held authority; and they wanted to substitute, not democracy, they wanted to substitute a Presbyterian Church. There were some elements of democracy, their priests, their presbyters, were to be chosen by their congregations; they did not want any bishops. It would be democratic, but a democratic church organization. But their aim and the aim of Cromwell and the Earl of Fairfax and the rest of them who started it, was to substitute a Presbyterian theocracy for the theocracy that ruled under Charles the First. There were other great issues at stake, commercial monopolies, parliamentary privileges, etc., but, nevertheless, they saw the thing fundamentally in theological terms. And they were not very strange in so doing, because two hundred years afterwards Gardner wrote a famous history of the Puritan Revolution in which he made it purely a religious affair. He has been discarded now, but he lasted quite a while.

The Civil War began between the gentry, the Presbyterian gentry, and the Monarchy and the supporters of the Monarchy, in 1640. By 1644 Charles was beaten. He kept his head on for five more years, but by 1644 he was militarily defeated. Why did he last so long? In order to defeat him the Presbyterians, the gentry, had had to call upon the common people, yeomen farmers and apprentices, to form Cromwell's famous Model Army. And when they had defeated the King and were looking around as to how they would establish a new regime, they found that the Model Army and the people whom they represented had different ideas as to what this regime was going to be, ideas different from the ideas of the Presbyterians. Their political name tells us a lot. They were called Independents. Independents because they did not want to be guided by priests or presbyters. Each man was ready to interpret Scripture independently.

The Presbyterian gentlemen began to look upon the King with a different eye. He did not look so bad after all, when now they could look back and see these monsters behind them. Charles also was very shrewd. He believed that he had been divinely appointed King. The Archbishop had anointed his head and he said, "Well, that's what I am; and these people who are doing this are treasonable, atheists, scoundrels, and in addition, I see they are in trouble with those who are behind them." He started to intrigue and maneuver. This went on from 1644 to 1646, and finally some of the men—captains, sergeants and others in the army, not the leaders, formed the Leveller Party. It is the first modern political party in the world, and it was formed practically by chance. It was formed, not against the King, but it was formed to deal with Cromwell, whom Lilburne, one of the leaders, had worshipped. Suddenly, between 1644 and 1646, they were faced with the fact that Cromwell was hesitating and Fairfax and the others, these Presbyterian noblemen and gentry, were ready to betray them. Out of this crisis sprang, in 1646, the Leveller Party. It had no serious antecedents; you can read and pick up something here and something there, and say that these were leading to it. You could always do that with new historical formations. But the party, as a party, was new, born in 1646, and by 1649 they had laid down the principles of parliamentary democracy. These were annual parliaments, almost manhood suffrage, payment of Members of Parliament, vote by secret ballot, equal constituencies, abolition of the House of Lords, abolition of the Monarchy, and sovereignty—the sovereignty of the nation resting, not with the King, or with the Parliament, but with the people. In about two years they had it all worked out, one of the greatest political achievements in the development of mankind. You see, they got it so clearly because they knew what they were fighting against. This and this and that and that had been going on and troubling them and they put up a proposition to meet each difficulty. That is how the people act when they do act. Yet the result was greater than anything you can find in Plato or Aristotle. Up to this day there are not many countries who are carrying out the parliamentary democracy that these fellows established between 1644 and 1646. They were so powerful that Cromwell had to compromise with them. But one day he was speaking in the House of Parliament, and Lilburne crept up to listen at the door and he heard Cromwell say: either we deal with these people or they are going to deal with us.

Cromwell used them to strike down the King's party. The King was executed, but shortly afterwards Cromwell destroyed the Leveller Party. He lasted for eleven years. Today, within the last fifteen or twenty years, some scholars—Haller, an American, and Davis, an Englishman— have been examining the works and writings of the period and general opinion is swinging to the view that if there had been any possibility of establishing a parliamentary republic in Britain around 1649 it was the way of the Levellers and not Cromwell's way. One cannot be sure of these things. I only give you an idea of what modern opinion is. The Levellers were very great men. They did a lot more than I am able to say here tonight. And one of them, Richard Overton, was the very prince of revolutionary journalists. To read him today is still a delight. And, most curious, many of the Levellers were known as Fifth Monarchy men. They said that the fifth monarchy St. John had written about, they were going to establish it.

By the way, I am told that some arrangements have been made for these lectures to be sold, or rather to be published for sale, which is rather different; so many of these references that I make I shall amplify when I correct the script.

So that is the way that the idea of parliamentary democracy came into the world. American teachers and writers preached for many generations that Jefferson and these had got their ideas from John Locke, an English philosopher, but I have noticed within recent years a great upsurge of interest in the Levellers, and recognition that they have more of the matter in them than Locke had.

Now just about this time, in the seventeenth century, when this is going on, we have one of the great discoveries in the intellectual development of mankind. You see, I put Shakespeare and the Levellers in that section. I put Shakespeare there for a particular reason. Shakespeare is the great dramatist of individual character. There is a great deal of debate as to what degree character really represents the essentials of his work. There is no need to go into that. The point was that individual characteristics, individual people in conflicts about individual problems, which they themselves were to settle, is what distinguishes Shakespeare's drama. It was symptomatic of the time.

## The Beginning of Modern Philosophy

And within that same period we have one of the great discoveries, the beginning of modern philosophy, in the work of Descartes, the Frenchman. There had been studies in astronomy and mechanics in particular going on for a number of years, and the old system of Ptolemy, the astronomical system of Ptolemy had been displaced by the system of Copernicus, not exactly displaced because in those days an astronomer, a scientist—it happened to Galileo, it happened to all of them—used to mix up his scientific discoveries with theological ideas. You were either proving that the church was right or proving that the church was wrong because it had not fully understood the greatness of God. Scientists would introduce moral values into the analysis of scientific matters.

This went on side by side with the development of astronomy, and investigation into mechanics and scientific progress were impeded by matters irrelevant to it.

In 1632, after twelve years of study, Descartes, the Frenchman, made a world-shaking pronouncement. His conclusion was as follows: "Look, I am tired of all these astronomers and scientists quoting Aristotle, quoting the Bible, quoting everything and mixing up scientific knowledge, so that a man does not know where to begin and where to end." He said, "*Cogito ergo sum*"—"I think, and therefore, I am." I think and therefore I exist. I know nothing else. God exists, but I know nothing at all about the world except what my intellect teaches me when I examine a subject. This was taking place about the same time as the revolution in Great Britain. You see, these things move in a certain pattern. The seventeenth century is the beginning of the modern world. At the same time, as out of the religious conflicts there breaks out at the end the Levellers with a political program, just about the same time, historically speaking, Descartes pulls the intellect out of all the mass of alien matters which had been obscuring its development, and he brings the intellect out plain and simple; from now on we are going to go by the mind, and this is what more or less dominates in Europe for another 150 years.

The last ones that I have on the list here are Tom Paine, Rousseau and the American and the French Revolutions; and with them I will bring the whole of this part to a conclusion. Descartes in France clears up the idea of the intellect. You can, by the way, still read his book today; it is short and it is very easy to read, and very fascinating. He calls it *A Discourse on Method*. Now we have to make a jump. In France the French Monarchy, by the middle of the eighteenth century, was quite degenerate. In England, in the seventeenth century, we have seen how the idea of parliamentary democracy sprang out of a struggle against a backward monarchy, a corrupt aristocracy and a clergy that was not in sympathy with the general ideas of the people. We find a similar situation in eighteenth-century France; and a group of Frenchmen, a good many of them followers of Descartes, decided that they would work against what existed in France.

The greatest of all propagandists was their leader, Voltaire. Voltaire called the whole thing, "l'infame." He gave it a name. You can translate it, "The Infamous." Today I think it will be better to translate it as, "The Mess." The whole lot of it—the Monarchy, the corrupt clergy, the aristocracy, "The Mess." "L'infame." He coined a slogan—"Ecrasez l'infame"—smash up The Mess. And wherever possible he ended what he wrote with "Ecrasez l'infame."

## The Age of Reason

These men, Voltaire, Diderot, D'Alembert, Grimm, believed that if you got rid of the superstition and the corruption and all the privileges which their corrupt rulers claimed, if you got rid of all that and used reason, just applied reason to human affairs, the result would be a happy, harmonious and progressive life for everybody. You see, the same problem—Plato and Aristotle, St. John of Revelations, the workers of the Middle Ages, and the men of the sixteenth century, the Englishmen of the seventeenth century. In the eighteenth century these Frenchmen were looking to reason to do it. They thought: "Well, in England they had a good constitution there, they have a king but he is reasonable; they have a government, a House of Commons and House of Lords; and we don't like the House of Lords too much, but by and large they seem very progressive. If we could only apply reason to our affairs and get rid of all this superstition and corruption, the prospects of a happy life would be with us." They did very well. They wrote remarkable books; they examined industry and science; they wrote philosophy; they analyzed and they preached. They published a great Encyclopedia, so that to this day they are called the Encyclopedists. They became world-famous. But trouble was ahead.

**Rousseau Rejects Pure Reason**

One of them was Jean-Jacques Rousseau, and after I recommend to you Aristotle—one or two books of his—in the whole of the period between Ancient Greece and the French Revolution, I certainly would recommend one writer, Rousseau, and one book of his, *The Social Contract*. Because Rousseau was an Encyclopedist with the others. He was a friend of Diderot and the rest. He studied with them, he worked with them, he wrote an article on music in the Encyclopedia; and then, suddenly, he said he was sitting down by the side of the road and he got a new idea which changed everything. Rousseau opened fire on the Encyclopedists. He said in effect: "You and your Age of Reason would be no better than all that is going on, that mess." Here was a crisis. Diderot, in particular, was cut to the heart, for after Voltaire, Rousseau was as sharp and as able a controversialist as any of them.

I am going to end this evening's session by giving you some idea of Rousseau's book, which is indispensable for modern political theory up to this very day. Rousseau had an original and independent mind and he set out to find the basis of government, a proper basis for government, and he says, "The first thing that we have to remember is that when we get together in society we do it upon the basis of a contract." Men got together and decided that they would pool their resources in order to have a type of society in which the liberty of each would become the liberty of all. "I, having given my liberty to a form of government, when I obey it, I am obeying myself. That is the social contract." But he went on to say that if at any time that government behaves in a manner contrary to our original agreement, then all allegiance to it ended, each man is on his own again. Now, that was a ferocious doctrine. Other men had written about the social contract before—Hume, Locke, Hobbes, but they had, most of them, made the contract in regard not only to the association of men but a contract in regard to government. Rousseau says the contract is not in regard to any government at all. He says the contract is between us, as people, to form a society; but we have no contract with any government; the contract is strictly between us, and the whole trend of this thought is that any time a government does not do what is satisfactory, we are finished with it; the contract is broken; we have to start all over again. That is a doctrine of profound revolutionary implications.

## He Repudiates Representative Government

But Rousseau is going to startle you still more. To this day he startles me, and I have been reading him for some forty years. Every now and then you see a sentence and you pull up. The Encyclopedists and the men of the Age of Reason were all concerned with a constitution and representative government. Rousseau thought that representative government was an absolute farce. He says the moment you vote and give your power to some other people, they begin to represent themselves or other interests, not the interests of the people. (laughter)

Rousseau thought that representative government deceived the people. And political parties too deceived the people. He said that as soon as political parties get together and start to quarrel with one another, all sorts of private or special interests come into play and the interest of the population is lost.

What does Rousseau recommend? And here, in my opinion, is the real greatness of his book. He knew what he wanted but he didn't know exactly how it could be translated into concrete political terms. He went round and round and in and out and in the end he did not succeed. But as history has gone on and you look you will see what Rousseau was driving at. He said there is something called "the general will"—the general will of the population. What is the general will? Is it when the population votes and there is a majority? He says, "No, it is not mere majority." He and other profound students of his work believe that if a minority merely has to obey a majority, that is tyranny. But he says if the majority expresses the general will, then the minority can obey, and that is not tyranny. How to get the general will? Rousseau cannot explain. Finally he says, "I think we should have a legislator, a legislator—a man who is able from ability and sensitivity to divine the general will and express it."

Rousseau is not easy because he does not shirk difficulties. But the more you study modern politics with a critical eye, the more you find in Rousseau.

People like Sir Ernest Barker and others say that Rousseau is totalitarian. It is an absurd statement altogether. No totalitarian has a social contract breathing down his neck which if it is not satisfied will burst the whole situation up. Rousseau is not a totalitarian; he is a revolutionary thinker, one of the greatest, and he was pointing his finger at the fundamental weaknesses of parliamentary and party government.

## What Can Replace Representative Government?

Now, what is it that Rousseau was really driving at? If you read *The Social Contract* you will see how often his references are to the Greek City-State. Rousseau, I am positive of this, is seeking a form of political organization in which the individual will feel himself in relation to a government in much the same way that the Greek citizen felt in relation to the City-State. And that is why he is not afraid of one man—a legislator—if that fellow will express the general will. But he is pretty sure that parliament and political parties as he has seen them will not express it. Once you put them there, they acquire, not through malice, not through vice—I am not speaking of the wickedness of men here at all, but from the objective circumstances—they acquire a life of their own which is separate from the life and the interests that they are supposed to serve. Most serious thinkers today will agree with him. The problem is to find a workable substitute. That is so difficult that many people who have no vested interest in representative government or party politics support them for want of a better.

I will end by this: much of our study of modern politics is going to be concerned with this tremendous battle to find a form of government which reproduces, on a more highly developed economic level, the relationship between the individual and the community, that was established so wonderfully in the Greek City-State. That was Rousseau's problem; he did not know the answer, but he stated the question. When the French Revolution came, it took the form that Rousseau had had in mind, and not the form of the men of the Age of Reason; and in the same way that after three or four years of civil war in England there broke out from the religious ideologies the political ideology, so the French Revolution, starting with the political ideology of the Rights of Man, after five or six years of civil war broke out with the socialism of Babeuf.

I have mentioned Thomas Paine. Paine was an Englishman. He went to America, he helped them with the American Revolution; he went to France, he helped them with the French Revolution, and he wrote various books—*Common Sense, The Age of Reason*, and *The Rights of Man*. And Paine (he is a very witty man, by the way, very sarcastic) gives you a readable idea of how the men of the Age of Reason thought. He is not a man of Voltaire's quality but he writes in English and if you read his books you get the Age of Reason pure and simple. And if you read *The Social Contract*, you see where the Age of Reason, despite its virtues, fell short.

My last word is that the leaders of the American Revolution established the idea of national independence. The French Revolution established the Rights of Man. Most of the gentlemen, by the way, of the eighteenth century were men of the Age of Reason—Jefferson, Washington, Madison and the others. I am informed, I have no reason to doubt it, that the first five Presidents of the United States were not Christians at all. They were all men of Reason. They believed in some sort of abstract God but not in any church. That was characteristic of the eighteenth century. These ideas dominated educated men of the eighteenth century. This body of thought played a great role. It is called the Enlightenment and the Illumination, and fittingly so. But what has endured from the eighteenth century is the man who challenged it from top to bottom, Jean-Jacques Rousseau. We are going to meet a lot of his ideas as we proceed. (applause)

# Chapter Two
## Thursday, 11th August, 1960

MR. "MYTHICAL"[1] CHAIRMAN, LADIES AND GENTLEMEN:

First of all, let me say how glad I am to see so many of the people who were present last time back again, and an audience quite comparable to the last one. My reason is this: I have no illusions at all as to the stiffness of the course that I am pursuing. I could have made it easier. It would have been less honest. Modern politics embraces all aspects of contemporary life. In order to understand the various ideas, the various solutions, it is my firm belief that we have to go back to where we began, and I am not going to back down. Last time I noticed at a certain stage that the strain of following what was, to some of you, a philosophical argument, was exercising a certain amount of pressure on you. It did you no harm, I am sure. It is true that I was taking a certain amount for granted, but what I am laying is a foundation and, as every lecture proceeds, I hope the foundation laid will become more and more part of the general movement forward. If I may venture a hint, I think by and large tonight would probably be the toughest of all. In the end we shall be in a better position to move faster because we shall have solid ground under our feet.

I would like to say a word, too, to those of the persuasion of my friend who raised the position of St. Thomas Aquinas and complained that I had not mentioned him. I am not doing a history of philosophy. If I were doing a history of philosophy, I would have to take up St. Thomas Aquinas and other Catholic theologians. I am trying to get at the foundations of modern politics and I am not aware that St. Thomas Aquinas and the doctrines that he preached are essential; in fact, I know they are not essential to my conception of modern politics. There is a university in

---

1   The Chairman was late.

the United States, a very powerful university too—Chicago University—where there are many Thomists, and the doctrines of St. Thomas are the basis of their approach to modern politics. That is theirs, that is not mine.

I would like to say, finally, that although I may appear to be calling some names and making brief references to them which does not validate the fact that they should be mentioned in the syllabus, they all have significance for where we are going, what we shall have to keep and what we shall have to discard.

Now I will say a word or two about what we did last time and then move on. We took up the Greek City-State; then we took up the Roman Empire. We followed with the towns, the City-States of the Middle Ages. We went on to the English Revolutions and then to the American and French Revolutions. It was a tremendous span. Nevertheless, each one of them showed at key moments in the history of the world the rise and decline of societies; what they contributed to the general stock of knowledge and learning and analysis about politics, and what were the ideas of the men who, at the time, made the records of those particular struggles and battles. So that at the end we were able to say that if we look at history in its key moments, there are many decades, and centuries, when nothing particular seems to have happened, and then a historical period stands up and strikes you as containing essential matter for further consideration.

## The Desire for Equality

Whenever masses of people saw a road open that they thought they could follow they have sought to establish a society of equality; a society of democracy. The great writers were preoccupied with it and it is noticeable that some of the greatest names in the history of political philosophy are precisely those writers who were seeking to establish, even if only in thought, a society of equality, harmony—all imbued with the idea of the progressive character of the life of mankind. I think I gave you evidence of that and it is worthwhile to know that we have that; that cannot, must not be challenged. We ended up, however, with the Age of Reason—those brilliant Frenchmen of the eighteenth century, and the challenge which one of them—you will remember, Rousseau—made to the doctrines of the Age of Reason, and I tried to make it clear that these men—Diderot, Rousseau, Voltaire, and the rest of them—were so convinced of the validity of reason because opposed to them there was the superstition of what I call "the corrupt monarchy"; not the clergy— I have always been careful to say "the corrupt clergy"—the clergy in France was very corrupt; and the parasitic aristocracy. Voltaire and these others believed that if you got rid of them and their superstition and their privileges and their claims to all sorts of special benefits in society, and substituted instead reason, the harmonious society, the progressive society and a society of a reasonable equality could be established.

Rousseau attacked this view. He attacked it before the French Revolution, and when the French Revolution came you had a startling example of "the general will," in that Robespierre carried the revolution through with extreme fierceness. In the end all reason and democracy and progress and equality and the Rights of Man—the French ruling classes, the aristocracy and the bourgeoisie—the capitalist class—said, "We have had enough of this. All this means nothing else but a lot of workers in the streets; strikes, making all sorts of impossible demands; we have had enough of it." And they put Napoleon in. That is how Napoleon was made the military dictator of France: it was for the purpose of finishing up with this democratic orgy which the French Revolution seemed to have unloosed. Napoleon found the French people the tallest race in Europe, but when he was finished with them in 1815, they were the shortest. It has been calculated that the amount of dead from military battles alone during the period of Napoleon's military career in Europe was some 3,700,000.

Now you can imagine all over Europe the progressive people, the intellectuals, the philosophers, the writers, the democrats—all looked upon the French Revolution as the time when the New World was beginning: reason would show itself as capable of solving the problems of mankind. Now it had ended in Napoleon and these desperate wars all over Europe. (That was not all there was to Napoleon, but as I say, we have to follow a certain discipline.)

## The Industrial Revolution

At this same time, the beginning of the nineteenth century, some years after the French Revolution, capitalism was establishing itself; the industrial revolution, that is to say, the application of science to industry, had begun its tremendous modern course. Adam Smith, one of the men of the Age of Reason, had been one of the first political economists to deal with it and the men who followed him, chiefly Sismondi and Ricardo, were horrified at what they saw capitalism was producing in society. It was quite clear that here was a process of creating wealth which the world had previously never seen; but at the same time it was quite obvious that it was creating conditions of disorder and misery among peasantry and workers which were out of all comparison with the enormous wealth that was accumulating in the hands of the capitalists and the owners. That early political economists were very much concerned with; and they wrote about it, and the ideas of democracy, equality, etc., ended in Napoleon and the socialism that had burst out in the last years of the French Revolution. Most of the men who attempted it had been put in jail, and the whole prospect was extremely bleak. In addition, there was another prospect that was disturbing the thinkers, the philosophers, the intellectual democrats at the time. They had no foundation under their feet, no intellectual foundation for such social and political ideas as they might have. The political philosophy of the eighteenth century had been blown to pieces by Rousseau and the French Revolution; and philosophy, logic, that analysis of ideas on which the Age of Reason had rested, that also was now in pieces. What to do? (The situation, by the way, was not very different from what ours has been since the Russian Revolution and what has happened since.)

Now Rousseau had attacked the Age of Reason. He had said: that kind of reason will not get you anywhere. And the great student of Rousseau—Kant—one of the greatest names in the history of Western civilization, had attacked the philosophical ideas which lay at the basis of the Age of Reason. And I must call upon you now for your close co-operation so that you can get some rough idea of the development of the European mind which led to the establishment of Marxism.

You will remember last time we said, somewhere about 1632 Descartes had established the primacy of the intellect. He said, "I think, therefore I am. That is all I know." But Descartes had followed Plato and endowed the mind with certain ideas innate to it. You know it was a tremendous thing to start with nothing else but the absolute mind, the pure mind, and yet be betrayed into thinking that the mind had certain ideas—this he had picked up from Plato. John Locke, the philosopher, opened fire on Descartes. He said, "These ideas that you think you have in your mind don't exist there at all. The mind is nothing; it is a blank piece of paper." Locke said that all we know is from experience. There is the world out there and things happen—the objective world, that is to say, the moon and stars and rivers and trees and societies and buildings and architecture and agriculture; that is the objective world out there. The mind is blank, the objective world makes impressions on the mind; that is about all. He says, "We get impressions; from these impressions we build up ideas." Locke was a great philosopher, an eminent political economist with various other qualifications, but he was fired at from both sides. He was fired at by Bishop Berkeley, a confirmed religionist, and he was fired at from the other side by David Hume.

Bishop Berkeley said, "You don't know anything about what is going on outside; you have no knowledge of it at all. This object today will seem to us hot and another instrument will measure it and say it is cold, and therefore the only guide we have is what is in the mind."

Berkeley did not hesitate. He said these ideas that we have in the mind came from God. And as if that was not bad enough, Hume on the other side said, "Well, Berkeley is right up to a point, although I don't believe that ideas come from God; they come from custom." He said the outside world hits the mind with a strong impression. That is a fact. It hits it with a weak impression and a weak impression is an idea; that is about all. He says in effect: "You can't possibly prove that the sun will rise tomorrow morning; you can't do that." And he is right. You can't. All you can say is that it has risen for so many thousand years every morning, so we can go to bed tonight prepared to get up and find it there next morning. He says, beyond that you cannot prove anything; and, he says, we really know nothing about the outside world. We have ideas about it, but we see something happen (his great word was "custom") and when we see, we get accustomed to something. We say, "If so and so," and, therefore, "so and so"; but he says it is not any idea of the mind, a capacity of the mind, it is just custom! We have seen it so often that we are able to draw the conclusion more or less.

Thus by the time Berkeley and Hume had finished with Locke, this mind, this reason, this philosophy on which the men of France had laid so much emphasis, philosophically and logically, was in ruins; there was nothing left.

## Kant

The man who made the first great attempt to solve the problem and give the mind some validity of its own in relation to the outside world was Kant, and the name of his book is very significant. It is *The Critique of Pure Reason*. He says this pure reason that all of you are working on wouldn't do. Kant says the mind has qualities of its own but they are not ideas at all. Every man is able to judge time and space; the time when a thing happened, what happened after that and the other thing that happened after. And space—where something is—he says that every human being born is able to judge time and space. Ask him, "Where did the mind get these qualities?" and he would probably have said, "Get out of my study. I cannot be bothered with you; the mind *must* have these two, time and space." He says the world is as difficult to understand as Hume and Berkeley said. We do not know anything exactly. All that we can know is what we get from our experience of it; we see something of the world. The world in itself. The thing in itself we don't know. Time and space in the mind enable us to make experiences. We get hold of certain phenomena and these phenomena the mind is able, basing itself on time and space and experience, to work out by intelligence, understanding. The mind draws certain principles; it can make certain discoveries, undoubtedly, which is what the men of the Age of Reason have done. You see, he had based this very solidly, the intelligence and the working on what time and space had got from the outside world, and there they—the men of the Age of Reason—had stopped. But Kant says, "As I look at the discoveries of the intelligence, as I look at what understanding and intelligence have worked out, I see signs of a more profound, of a deeper and more embracing logic; a more embracing body of ideas. In other words, the objective world, time and space, gets impressions; it works out, intelligence works out some ideas. "But when I examine those ideas," says Kant, "there is more in it than what came from outside." He says, "I seem to be expressing a tremendous body of deeper, more profound, more extensive, more complex ideas. So that Reason, as we saw it, was both the result of the examination of what we got by experience from the external world and also the translation by the human intellect working on it, but also there is something else which is not connected with the external world at all, and this I call Reason." And if you had asked him, "What is this Reason, do you know it? Does it exist?" He would have said,

"I don't know. But what I am doing here I need in order to make sense out of the mind. In addition to what I get from outside by experience there is something else. Pure Reason as you all have used it is not enough."

Kant had published *The Critique of Pure Reason* before the French Revolution. It is very noticeable that Kant had learned from Rousseau. It is too complicated to go into here, but Kant had learned from Rousseau. In the modern world, wherever you go and you find something striking, you trace it back and you find that Rousseau had something to do with it. Kant acknowledges his debt to Rousseau quite plainly.

## Hegel

After the French Revolution the great school of German philosophers, which begins with Kant, works at these problems and ends in the man who, in my opinion, and in the opinion of Marxists, brought philosophy to an end—Hegel. And his history is most dramatic.

Hegel had studied Christianity; he had studied the Greek City-State; he was reading Sismondi and particularly Ricardo. He was a great student of Kant. With all this in his mind he was working out a philosophy, and we have his early notes. How was he to solve the problem? What was this Reason that Kant had written about? The French Revolution, what had it attempted? The problems that Ricardo and Sismondi and these others were posing with regard to the new capitalist society; the equality of all men, which had been established by Christianity. He was a great student of Christian theology and the City-State of Greece, and he was working out a philosophy; and we have today, within recent years, his early manuscripts. In them we see that young Hegel reached a stage where, if he had gone on, he would have been compelled to say that the only solution to these problems was the proletariat establishing a new regime and laying the basis of human equality. What is most striking is that just as he reaches there, the manuscript breaks off and he does not write any more. He just couldn't do it. Later we will talk about why.

## Marx

Instead he developed a tremendous philosophical method—dialectic. We cannot go into that now. We will go into that later, but what I want to make clear is that the step that Hegel reached, the stage that Hegel approached and could not achieve, thirty years afterwards, Marx, a great student of Hegel and a young Hegelian in his youth, student of Ricardo, student of Greek philosophy (his doctoral thesis was on a conflict between two different types of Greek philosophical writers), Marx made the step that Hegel had been unable to make thirty years before. Marx says that this Reason that Kant was talking about and Hegel had developed (he called it world-spirit) was the developing consciousness of mankind seeking to establish a harmonious society. He says, now, as I tried to show last time, men have always attempted but failed. Now, with capitalism, it is at last possible. The tremendous wealth of the capitalist society and with its combined organization and degradation of the proletariat, that offers the opportunity to do what men have been trying to do over these centuries. The new political doctrine of Marx was not the doctrine of the age of the men of Reason; it was not the doctrine of Rousseau either. It sprang from the socialism which evolved at the last stage of the French Revolution (which was still the greatest event in European history). So that Marx claims (and we Marxists claim, and are very proud of this) that we did not come from a corner or some hole; that Marx was not somebody who was suffering, as a psychoanalyst will tell you, from some neurosis, that he was a Jew and he hated society and that is why he wrote this theory. Not at all. Marx could claim in the year 1848, "I wrote *The Communist Manifesto* as a result of many years of study by which I solved the problems which had been posed by French socialism, which had been posed by the political economy of Adam Smith and Ricardo, and by the philosophical analysis of Kant and Hegel; I carried to its conclusion, the work that had been begun by Descartes since the 17th century." He could claim that Marxism was the solution and the heir to the finest currents of thought and action of five hundred years of European history.

## The Inheritance of Marxism

You know there are people who say, "I don't like the dictatorship of the Left and I don't like the dictatorship of the Right—Hitler and Stalin." Hitler's doctrine was based on the throwing back of Europe to the mentality of people before the Renaissance. He said that the abolition of slavery in the United States was a mistake; it should never have been done. His doctrines were the doctrines of blood and race, and as far as religion was concerned he tried to restore the worship of Odin, Thor and those other gods of the ancient Norse. How is it possible for a modern educated man who has studied Marxism at all and modern political philosophy, to speak of the dictatorship of the Right and the dictatorship of the Left as if they are both the same? In day-to-day controversy you have to deal with it because you have to deal with your opponents, but outside of that these people are beneath contempt. That is the first thing to establish. Marxism is the culmination of the most important currents of five hundred years since the Renaissance of European thought and social and political action. We have to remember Hume. That long ancestry does not prove that it is right. You cannot prove logically that Marxism is right. It will prove itself right when it shows what it is able to do. At any rate, anybody with any intellectual pretensions or ideas of understanding politics has to make himself familiar with Marxism, to understand it and not be frightened by the shouts from reactionaries everywhere who, the moment you say "Marx," say "Communism" . . . (words drowned out by applause)

Now, I have to go on further and show you what perhaps you are more familiar with. Marx wrote *The Communist Manifesto* in 1848 and established the First International in 1864. From that time up to 1917, the history of Western Europe is the history of the struggle between the supporters of a capitalist society on the one side, and on the other, supporters of Marxism. That is fact, and if we take it up to the present day, from 1917 to today, the history of the whole of modern society is the history of those who are mobilized under the banner of capitalism, welfare state or whatever it is, and those who are mobilized under the banner of Marxism. I am very hostile to the particular brand of Marxism that is dominant today. Nevertheless, in the contemporary world today we have Russia with two hundred million people and carrying on a tyrannical rule over I don't know how many. We have China with six hundred million claiming to be Marxists. So that Marxism does not only claim that it sums up in itself centuries of historical, social and political philosophical developments. Today, in 1960, we go further; we say however weak, however disappointing, however reactionary, nevertheless this policy, this doctrine that was put forward in 1848 and made such claims for itself in the past as to its ancestry today, after 112 years, those claims objectively, in the historical development, in the actual state of politics and economics before us, that doctrine has justified a claim—I am going to be very modest—at least to be studied and be respected.

## The 1848 Revolution in France

It is really most exciting, the pursuit of thought, because Rousseau had challenged the age of Reason before the French Revolution showed up its weaknesses. Kant had challenged the basis of their thought before the French Revolution showed that the thought had no sound basis. Marx, early in 1848, had written *The Communist Manifesto* talking about social-ism as the future society, but the great revolution had not yet taken place. I think Marx published in February, and in April the revolution broke out in France; and this was a strange one. You see, the French workers had been out in 1789, in Paris in particular. They were out again in '91. In '92 they established the republic. They were out again in '93; twice in '95, and then Napoleon put an end to them; before he fought the enemy abroad he dealt with the enemy at home.

In 1830 there was another revolution in France.

After all these experiences the Parisian workers came to a general conclusion. They said, "You know this democratic republic for which we always made the revolution does not seem to suit us, because whenever we make it, while there is a lot of talk about freedom and liberty and equality for everybody, in the end we are very much where we were before. A new set of people are in, usually those who did not fight in the streets; they are sitting there and we, who shed our blood and took the risks, have got nothing from it."

So that they came to the conclusion that this 1848 revolution was to give them a new kind of republic. What kind of republic? Engels and Marx who followed the thing very closely said later, "When you asked them they did not know, but it was not to be the democratic republic, it was to be a socialist republic." What did they mean? They did not know exactly; it was very pathetic; they said, well, there must be workshops where the unemployed can go and get work. That is the only idea that they put forth, but they were quite clear that it was not a democratic republic they wanted but a socialist republic. They were serious. In June they took arms in hand to establish it. They were defeated and massacred and driven back into their homes, and the French bourgeoisie did exactly what it had done after the French Revolution. It put another Napoleon in power—finished up with all this democracy: these monstrous workers were not only talking about democracy and freedom but they wanted a special republic of their own. That wouldn't do. Napoleon finished with all this.

Now I mentioned de Tocqueville, and for a particular reason I want you to remember de Tocqueville's name. De Tocqueville was a Frenchman who lived around the same time as Marx and he is famous for two books, one on the French Revolution, and one on democracy in America, and you have to go to the United States and live there for some time to realize the extraordinary penetration that de Tocqueville showed in writing about America 130 years ago. Time and again he writes as if he is talking about people whom you have just met in the subway or somewhere else. De Tocqueville looked at 1848 *and he came to much the same conclusions as Marx did*, only he was on the opposite side; and it is worthwhile reading today—at least I and my friends find him instructive because he saw what took place in 1848.

## The Dictatorship of the Proletariat

Marx studied the whole process of 1848 very closely, and in writing about it he used the phrase which is still the subject of bitter controversy to the present day. He said the socialist republic that these workers wished to establish is nothing more nor less than a dictatorship of the proletariat. When he was asked: what is this dictatorship of the proletariat, he would not answer. Now there is no need to be coy about it today. I am going to spend a few minutes on getting that phrase, which creates such passion when it is used, on getting it clear. Marx point of view was that in an economic society like capitalism, although you might form labor parties, and win reforms, and at certain times you might even win electoral victories, at all critical moments the dominant economic class was certain to impose its will upon those who were fighting against it; and he said that capitalist society meant, in essence, fundamentally, the dictatorship of the bourgeoisie, the domination of the capitalist class, as the ruling class in the particular type of economy. This rule might take the form of a brutal oppressive dictatorship such as was Napoleon's. It might take the form of a constitutional monarchy, as in Britain, and it might take the form, as it did for many years in the United States, of a democracy. "But," Marx says, "whether it was a near totalitarian government or a constitutional monarchy or free democracy, in the last analysis all represented the dictatorship of the bourgeois class."

"Now," Marx goes on to say, "if the proletariat established a socialist society, this society might take the form of an extreme dictatorship; it might take the form of an extremely wide and far reaching democracy. That was not the point. The conception of a dictatorship of the proletariat means that at all critical moments the will of the class which dominates the economic system, i.e., the proletariat, will prevail. That is all."

Marx was firmly of the belief that a socialist society would be ushered into existence through the democratic republic. He did not believe that the establishment of a socialist society would have to pass through a stage of dictatorship in the usual sense of that term.

## The First Communist International

What infuriated his political enemies is that he would not explain the term. In 1864 he formed the First International. It was a Marxist International. The organizer of it, the writer of its political documents, was Karl Marx. It gained rapid supporters in Britain, in France, in Italy, and many parts of Europe. And here is something to remember: for the first time in some five hundred years, Europe once more had a doctrine and a leader who commanded the allegiance, direct or indirect, of millions of Europeans. Marxism did not come from a corner; neither has it lived in holes and corners. The last time that had happened in Europe was in the Crusades when hundreds of thousands of people had gone off to save the Holy Land from the Saracens and to punish the Saracens for their sacrilege by taking as much of their land as possible. After the Crusades, that was over. Europe did not know another international social or political organization or doctrine organized around a single figure until Marx founded the First International in 1864 with the rapid response in Britain and the rest of Europe. Such was the First International. It came to an end with the Paris Commune in 1871 and we have to spend a little time on the Paris Commune because it will teach us a great deal about the Marxist doctrine and the Marxist method.

## The Paris Commune

There was war between France and Germany. France was defeated and in the confusion the Paris workers threw over Napoleon the Third and established a democratic socialist republic. It lasted 71 days. (When the Russian Revolution of October 1917 reached the 72nd day, Lenin said: we have beaten them by one day—this is progress.) The importance of the Paris Commune is this: it was not a Soviet; it had no Workers Councils; it did not nationalize anything; it was elected by ordinary suffrage; it was a plain election and the result was the Paris Municipal Council, so to speak. But the workers had learned a great deal between 1848 and 1871.

In 1871 the Council that was elected at the Paris Commune made a tremendous political step forward, although it lasted for only 71 days. The leaders declared that the Council would be both executive and legislative in one. You see, all previous governments that practiced democracy had established legislation by means of the parliament and then handed it over to government—the executive—to carry it out. A whole lot of time had been spent in working out the various proportions between the legislative, the executive and the judiciary: how much power for each, who would control whom, etc. The Commune established a new principle: legislative and executive in one. Remember it. We shall meet it again.

## The Second International

In 1889 the Second International was formed with millions of members this time—Marxists—a Marxist International. Furthermore, the trade unions of Europe now joined together in a Trade Union International whose guiding ideas were also Marxist. The history of modern Europe is the history of the mobilization of the proletariat under the banner of Marxism to overthrow the capitalist society and establish socialism. These Internationals were not the work of a few people or a few politicians. You see, sometimes in a colonial country, a Communist is a strange fellow. He walks along the road and people point him out, "You see, he is one of them . . ." (laughter) Whenever he goes to speak somewhere, the police go after him. "Tell the people, warn everybody; you had better not listen, you know! He may mean well but . . ." (words drowned out by applause)

Yet you cannot write the history of Western Europe, particularly from about 1889, without writing the history of Marxism. There are two forces: the international socialist movement and the international trade union movement. [Lecturer removes his coat and comments: "It is extremely hot. I hope you don't mind. We are dealing with, after all, revolutionary politics!" (laughter)]

So that between 1889 and 1914 on the one hand you have various capitalist societies, and by 1914 you have millions of workers organized in the Second International and many more millions of trade unionists organized in the International Trade Union Movement, all dedicated to the overthrow of capitalist society, the establishment of socialism according to the ideals and principles of scientific socialism, the doctrines of Marx and Engels. These are the facts.

Now we have reached to 1914 and we can stop there and go over to the United States.

## The American Development

In this hall already I have spoken of why the Civil War was fought. The Civil War was fought, not to free slaves. There must be no misunderstanding about that. By the way, I do not blame people for not choosing to leave their comfortable homes in order to free slaves. People just don't do that sort of thing. (laughter) If governments want to make a war, they will tell you they are defending gallant little Belgium or they have made a treaty with Poland and they must keep the treaty with Poland; or they have to defend the principles of democracy. They invent all these beautiful reasons because the masses of people on the whole are idealistically inclined and like to feel that if they have to go to war it is to make the world a better place than it was before; that is undoubtedly true. But the political leaders do not go in for war on those principles; and the North did not fight the South to free the slaves. What happened was that the South, owing to its climatic and regional structure had slavery and the North had not. There was a constant conflict between them, normal political conflict. Then about 1850, the modern world was beginning. It was clear that if you take this line to be the Mississippi, it was clear that the next stage in the development of the United States was the expansion and industrialization and population of the whole of the West. And the

Civil War was fought over who was to do this. Because if the Southern states, with their slave economy, dominated the West, it meant that they would be more powerful in the Federal Government in Washington and they would develop the life and society of the United States in their own way. And the North said, "We are not going to sit down here and see you take all this territory and make it into slave states." And Lincoln said, "What you have down there, slavery, I don't like, but you can keep it. However, no more slavery over this way. This is going to be a territory for free states." The South seceded and the war began.

Take Ohio and Minnesota, those Scandinavian states. They did not want to see a Negro around there; they chased them out whenever they came. "We do not want Negroes here. They only make a lot of trouble." They were against the South because their goods went down the Ohio and down the Mississippi to the sea, and they were not going to have an independent South in control of the mouth of the Mississippi and half of the United States. So that they were determined to see to it that the South was brought back in the Union and the whole country controlled by the Federal Government; but as for the Negroes, they did not want them up there.

But there is no doubt that as the war went on, popular sentiment grew, and Lincoln said, "We will fight it to the end." That is undoubtedly true. We need not exaggerate one side or the other. The Civil War was fought and America started to expand.

## Melville, Whitman and Mark Twain

I have mentioned Herman Melville and Whitman, the two greatest writers of the United States; and Herman Melville's great book, *Moby Dick*, is the outline of society as he saw it in the future. For him, the future development of world society was the totalitarian society. There is, to my mind, no question about that. But he did not only write it in the form of fiction. Melville wrote in one of his books, "Look, America has democracy, it has freedom; it is not like that miserable continent, Europe. But," he adds, "the moment that the West has been built up and industrialized with a full population, and the whole of America is as full of people as Europe, all that is taking place in Europe is going to take place here."

Whitman's mind was not so penetrating. Everyone knows Whitman today as the man who wrote and spoke with great eloquence and poetic power of the grandeur of America, of the democracy of America, the future of humanity in American democracy, etc. But that was not the Whitman of about twenty years after. Walt Whitman died with the gloomiest perspectives of the future of democracy in the United States. (When I want to speak about the gloomy perspective of democracy in the United States, I am going to point out loudly and clearly, "I say so." But at the present time, I am pointing out what was the view of Walt Whitman.) (laughter) It was the view of Whitman; it was the view of Melville; it was the view of the great humorist, Mark Twain. Despite the great burst of industrial development, the finest minds in the United States were very doubtful of the future of democracy. They were not Marxists, but they saw below the surface and they stated their ideas and left them for us to ponder over. We will look at those ideas again.

## Prelude to World War I

And now we come to what I call "Surplus capital" and "Made in Germany" and this is the last point that I have to make because the next one flows directly from it. The world today is dominated by the threat and the fear of war. It is the threat of war which dominates the economies of the great nations; it is the threat and fear of war which dominates their politics; it is the threat and the fear of war which dominates the psychology of ordinary minds. That being so, the causes and the course of the two world wars that we have had are of extreme importance to all who are studying politics; and I want briefly to put before you a certain method—a basic map, so to speak—of what took place between, say, 1900 and 1917. This must be the basis of our further investigation into contemporary politics.

Great Britain for 200 years has followed out a policy of "the balance of power" in Europe. No country in Europe would be allowed to dominate the continent because that would put the defense of Britain in an impossible position. They had fought against Louis XIV. They had fought against Napoleon, and in 1914 they went to war against the Kaiser for that purpose and that purpose only. It nearly had been different, because, if you want to preserve the balance of power, you can fight with A against B, or you can fight with B against A. And some time towards the end of the century there were elements in Britain who said that it was better to join up with Germany instead of joining with Russia and France. That fell through. The *Entente Cordiale* was established and when the war came it came against Germany and the Central Powers.

## "Made in Germany"

Below this business of the dominant power in Europe, tangled up with it, was the question of new developments, not only in political, but in industrial and commercial relations. Some of you are too young—most of you are too young to remember—I remember it as a small boy before the war: "Made in Germany." British colonies were being flooded with goods made in Germany. Today they are being flooded, I think, with goods "Made in Japan." Isn't that so? In addition, there was competition for the continent of Africa.

In 1880 when they were all scrambling for Africa, Bismarck summoned the Treaty of Berlin and there they had sat down around the table and comfortably carved up Africa. "I will take that; you take that, and you take that." My friends, that is exactly what happened. They divided it among themselves. By 1914, some of the weaker ones—like Germany in 1880—felt they were more powerful now; they wanted a larger share of Africa. The thing had to be redivided, and you can divide with a certain amount of peace, but redivision is something else; so that you see you have a complex of conflicts: Britain, to keep the balance of power in Europe; Britain and Germany fighting over world markets; all of them squabbling over the redivision of Africa. There was the question of where to export surplus capital. That is treated in many books, the best of which is Lenin's *Imperialism.*

Everybody could see the war coming but they could do nothing to stop it. The Second International, consisting of socialist workers from Germany and France and Britain and Belgium and Holland and Russia, etc., met at an international conference in 1907 and decided that they would not take part in any imperialist war. When the war came and their rulers were inciting them, they would say, "No, we are not going to fight against our proletarian brothers; the war we are going to fight is against you for leading us into this mess." This was in 1907. Five years afterward the drive to war was becoming stronger and stronger. The international socialists met again in 1912 and they passed another powerful anti-war resolution.

## The Failure of the Second International

You know, when we look back, it should give us cause for thought. Here the world in 1914 was moving into this period of war and disaster—the degradation of civilization which has continued unabated til the present day. The Marxist International met in 1907 and then met again in 1912 and pledged themselves to resist it to the end by holding a united front against the international quarrels of the rulers of the various countries. My friends, in 1914, when the war broke out, they were unable to stick to it; they broke down and each went with the rulers and the armies and the politicians of his own country. But today, as I look back, the anger and the hostility with which we looked upon them as having betrayed the cause, do not now loom so largely in my own mind. Looking back at 1907 and that resolution of theirs, and 1912 and their resolution and then their breakdown in 1914—as I look back there from 1960, today, I see them as spineless, it is true, and many of them had paid only lip service to Marxism. But they were the initiators of a great international movement, which, in my opinion, more than ever today is the only solution to the perils and catastrophic destruction which faces society. That we shall come to.

They broke down in 1914, the Marxist International. They went to war. They led the workers into the war. But the vitality of the Marxist movement was proved by the fact that the moment it became clear to one of them, Lenin, that the International had broken away from the principles and the policies that it had proclaimed, he set out at once to lay the foundation of the Third International, and it was under the banner of the Third International that the Russian Revolution took place in November 1917 and, ultimately, brought the European war to a close. That is what I mean by 1848 to 1917. We have come right through: We have seen what Marxism has behind it, and we are now by 1917 in the midst of what Marxism has before us. (applause)

# Chapter Three
## Monday, 15th August, 1960

MR. CHAIRMAN, LADIES AND GENTLEMEN:
We have so far covered a certain amount of ground and I hope that those who are following are now more or less confident that, although we jumped from spot to spot as people jump from rock to rock in crossing a river, nevertheless we were laying certain foundations.

## A Review

In the first lecture, I made it clear that at critical moments when the great masses of people, who usually are not particularly active in politics, see an opportunity to shape the course of political events, they usually, or they have often attempted to establish a society of equality, of harmony and of progress. We saw, also, that the writers who wrote round and about those events themselves were moved by the desire, if possible, to work out in theory what, at critical moments, the masses tried to do in practice. It is obvious that what I said in that period cannot be considered the history of political evolution. There are long periods in history when nothing particular happens in the sense that there is nothing outstanding for the historian or analyst of the future. A revolution, however, is important because at that time, all pretenses and conventions are torn away and you see social reality. In taking the Greek City-State, the Roman Empire, the City-States of the Middle Ages, the English Revolution and the French Revolution and the American Revolution, I believe I took a representative body of events. Later we went on to deal with the more modern developments in politics.

Modern politics begins, apart from the leap to political democracy of the Levellers, with the men of the Age of Reason. What they did is still viable in modern politics. But it was limited. We saw how Rousseau, in political philosophy, and Kant, in philosophy proper, attacked the ideas of the men of Reason—the men of the eighteenth century—and how the French Revolution showed that Rousseau and Kant had a firmer grasp and deeper penetration into political reality than the other men of the eighteenth century had, despite the good work that they had done. The eighteenth century looked forward to the revolution (although the revolution that actually took place was not the one that had been expected. They would have been horrified at it, but revolutions have that habit). The revolution took place. It ended in Napoleon, and this disappointment unloosed a crisis in the thought of Western civilization. Out of that crisis emerged the philosophy of Hegel, the political economy of Sismondi, Ricardo and others, and then, finally, out of the struggle to find a substitute for what the Age of Reason obviously had been unable to do, we get Marxism. The details you can work out, you will have to work out for *yourselves*. The important thing is to get firm hold of the movement of ideas and the developing sequence of events.

## The General Direction

My reason is this. The eighteenth and nineteenth centuries were dominated by the idea of progress. Human society was seen as a progressive evolution with many retreats and deviations to one side and sometimes long periods of undistinguished bleakness; nevertheless, the general attitude in the eighteenth and nineteenth centuries was that mankind was making progress towards some future in which man would arrive at some sort of society that corresponded to his special status in the universe. The twentieth century has seen such a decay and degeneration in modern society that now the idea of progress, except among the Marxists, is in decay; it is sneered at and it is denounced by many excellent people. In other words, they repudiate the whole of the eighteenth and nineteenth centuries. The present crisis of mankind in the twentieth century is the most disturbing in the history of human society. If we continue to believe in the idea of progress, and not only to believe but to carry out our politics within the orbit of that idea, it is necessary, particularly at this time, that we know where we have come from and the foundations upon which we stand. Progress is not in a straight line. (Rousseau had some startling ideas on progress.) But the general direction is clear.

Last time, having shown the foundations and the origins of Marxism, I proceeded to take up the First, the Second and the beginning of the Third International, all of them different stages in the progressive evolution of the working class. I stated without any equivocation that the history of Europe since 1848 to the present day, after World War I to a great degree, and substantially after World War II, is fundamentally a history between the defenders of capitalism and official society and the attack upon this society by people who are organized under the banner of Marxism. This is not a question of whether you agree with Marxism or not. I stated, and I state it again, that the history of Europe since 1848 to the present day, and particularly since World War II when the Far East is included, is the history of the struggle between traditional capitalist society and those who are attacking it under the banner of Marxism. If you do not accept that, if you do not see that, then you can belong to a political organization, and you can carry out political activity, but you have no conception of what is the course of modern history. Those who claim to be Marxists are divided. You know where I stand. But without that general picture you are lost.

Now tonight I am going to proceed along much the same lines. I am not giving you a history of any period. I am trying to outline a course of development, so that when you look back at your past reading or you undertake new, at any rate you will have some idea of the general line which many others besides myself follow. And so we come to Lenin and the Third International, the Russian Revolution.

## Socialism and Communism

Now someone last week asked me what was the difference between the Socialists and the Communists. I have described the Second International—masses, millions of them, organized in their various labor parties (the official name is Social Democratic); and these same millions organized in the International Trade Union Movement, and that was the organization of the working class in its essential and most advanced elements up to World War I. As you remember, they had decided to oppose imperialist war and each section of the international proletariat was to maintain its internationalism by attacking the capitalists in its own country. They passed that resolution in 1907, they passed it again in

1912 and when the war came in 1914 they broke down and, substantially, each went along with its own national forces. In 1917, however, Lenin, who had opposed this from the start—it is quite significant that he was an exile from Russia—when he heard the news that the German Social Democracy, which was the parent of all these movements, had supported the war policy of the Kaiser and his government, Lenin disbelieved it. He said, "This is nothing else but war propaganda and fakery"; but it turned out to be true. They all had gone their individual nationalistic way. Lenin did not. In 1917 the revolution broke out in Russia and Lenin was able to go back home, assume its leadership and lay the foundations for a Third International.

Soon after the war was over, the working class movement in the great countries of Western Europe found itself divided into two—those who continued to be "national" and to believe that socialism would come by gradual and parliamentary ways, and those who went with Lenin and decided that socialism could come only by the violent over-throw of the bourgeoisie. The Communists linked themselves in an international organization, the Third International. They said that the Second International had betrayed socialism. And to the present day the workers of Europe, wherever there is freedom of political organization, are divided into these fundamental groups: the Second International, preaching that parliamentary democracy, universal suffrage and votes will bring socialism; the Communist International, guided, organized by Moscow, devoted in theory to the idea of revolution, but working as one single group for the establishment of international Communism. That is the basic disagreement. In between you have all sorts of left democrats, and half-Communists and Trotskyites, etc., but these are small and if, at any time, they come to some importance, we will hear about it.

In addition, the Second International has its own trade union move-ment and the Third International has its own trade union movement. There are new developments in Africa; we will come to those in time.

## The Soviet Form

Now the important thing about the Russian Revolution—I am not going into the cause of the revolution at all—is the fact that it initiated for the first time—brought into being—the Soviet form, the Soviet which appeared in the 1905 Revolution in Russia, which had failed. What is the Soviet? The Soviet is nothing more than a political organization which is elected by 500 workers, more or less, in every factory. So that the Moscow Soviet consists of workers who are elected not as in ordinary political democracy, as single individuals, according to their place of residence, but as members of an organization of production—a factory or any place where workers are congregated. They elect and you have the city Soviet, the Moscow Soviet. You have the regional Soviet, the Soviet of the Ukraine and you have the All-Russian Soviet. Now the thing that we have to remember always is *that nobody invented it. Nobody organized it. Nobody taught it to the workers.* It was formed spontaneously and in fact when it was formed in 1905 the two divisions of the Russian Social Democratic Party both turned up their noses at it, and Lenin had to come from abroad and tell them: "Why don't you go in? Go in."

Now up to 1917 Lenin had not had the slightest idea of establishing socialism in Russia, none at all. He said: "This is a backward country. It has about two million workers; it has over 100 million peasants—socialism in this country is an absurdity. You can talk about socialism when you have a majority of industrial workers—that is the basis of socialism. For Russia of 1917, impossible."

We have that today in Britain, in France and Germany, in Holland, certainly Italy, Spain, etc. But in 1914–1917, with this mass of peasantry—a backward, ignorant peasantry, great illiteracy, Lenin said, "What we can do is to carry the bourgeois-democratic revolution through, establish parliamentary democracy and finish off with the landlords, the corrupt clergy and the czars. Then the capitalists of Russia will come into power. We cannot help that. We will become a Socialist Opposition for the time being."

Revolutionary history in England and in France shows that to get the bourgeoisie into power, the workers have to do it. The bourgeoisie are not able to do that themselves; they talk a lot but when it comes to fighting they are not too eager. They are not cowards but as soon as they see the mass of the people in the streets, and organizing themselves, the bourgeoisie starts to make compromises with the feudal reactionaries. That is why Lenin said that we, the proletariat, have to carry the bourgeois democratic revolution through to a conclusion, but once we have carried it through we are not strong enough to maintain or even to establish a socialist society. What they were going to have in Russia is what existed then in France, Britain, Germany, etc. They were ready for socialism. Russia was not.

If Lenin had new and rigid and very severe ideas about the organization of his party which we have come to know as the Leninist Party, it was because Russia was a police state. This being so, the Russian party could not function freely as the others where there was no police state. Russia had to have a very disciplined party to fight a police state. These were the ideas of Lenin up to 1917.

## Lenin and the Soviets

The first revolution in Russia broke out in March, and if you read one or two of his early letters you will see that he had much the same ideas even after he had the first news of the revolution; but later the news came over, not only about the political problems of Russia—I can't go into that—but about the Soviet. Within about 72 hours after the overthrow of Czarism, 20 million workers in Russia were organized in Soviets in all the large cities of the country.

Lenin took a new position. He said nobody told the Russian workers to do that; nobody taught them to do that. They were not instructed; nobody expected it. Here they had built up these organizations that were actually in charge of the various cities of Russia. If they had wanted parliamentary democracy, they would have organized themselves differently.

Lenin recognized that this was one of those creative events that occur very rarely in history. It is nearly always spontaneous, this creation of a new political form. What clinched it was that on all the urgent questions—end the war, land to the peasants etc.—the new government, which would be swept out of power by the Bolsheviks in October, was opposed to the Soviets.

Thus when Lenin came to Russia he said, "All power to the Soviets." There was a row not only among other people but inside his own party. They told him, "For all these years you have said that Russia is only suited to bourgeois parliamentary democracy. You have said Britain and the others will form a socialist society. But we have to wait behind." He answered, "What are you going to do with these Soviets? This means the people are ready for socialism. We must go forward."

The Soviets were the new form and it was through the Soviets that Lenin went on to power. When the Bolshevik Party took power, it nationalized nothing. It is the workers who went on and nationalized. Lenin did not want to nationalize anything. If you read Lenin's writings closely you will see that from 1917 to 1923, that is, about 71 months, I think I have counted—and I can't read Russian—that about 90 times he told the Russians, "We cannot have any socialism here; you had better take note of that." There were times when he said, "We will be lucky if our children and our children's children get socialism. All we can do is to hold on to the proletarian power and hope that in Germany and Britain and France the workers will succeed. If they succeed, we are safe; if they don't, we are lost." He was a very harshly realistic man. Nobody ever said anything half as savage about the Russian Soviet State as Lenin himself said, but if you, an enemy, attacked the Soviets, he would go to town on you and say, "I am entitled to say these things, not you."

So there was the Soviet State formed in Russia, formed on the basis that nothing else could have satisfied the demands of the people, but on the expectation that the rest of Europe would follow. Lenin said over and over again: "If they in Europe don't achieve another socialist revolution, we in Russia are lost."

## The Dictatorship of the Proletariat

Now we are going to look for a bit at the Soviet State—the Soviet form. You will remember where we began in 1848. The workers in Paris were saying, "We don't like this democratic republic because after we have come out into the streets and overthrown the reaction, the end of the democratic republic is that we are left holding the bag; we get nothing. So we want a new republic, a socialist republic." And Engels, who writes the history of this period, says, "When you asked them what was the socialist republic, they did not know." All they knew was that they did not want the old one, they wanted a new one.

Marx examined this and he said the next workers' revolution is going to establish the dictatorship of the proletariat. People asked him what was the dictatorship of the proletariat. He would not answer. Then came the Commune. Now observe closely how the Commune came. It came by ordinary suffrage, manhood suffrage; it was an ordinary election, but the government that was elected made a great step forward, from the Marxist point of view. They said, "This Legislature is going to be legislative and executive at one and the same time," and Marx, who worked from what had happened, comparing it with what existed before, and then upon this basis speculating as to what is likely to take place in the future, Marx said: "It looks as if you can't take over a state of bourgeois parliamentary democracy or any bourgeois state, put socialists in it and so create a socialist state. You see what happened in the Commune? They rejected entirely the bourgeois state, and they made a state for themselves."

It lasted only 71 days, and Marx must have spent God knows how many hours working out and examining and seeing what was involved. Lenin and other Marxists studied Marx and they studied society. Thus when the Soviet broke out in 1917 it was clear to them that a new stage had been reached, because the Soviet was a political form based on the economic units and economic relations in society. (Later there were peasant Soviets.) Marxism had laid it down that any society, in its social and political relations, could only be properly explained by examining its economic basis. And here these Russian workers—the majority of them knew nothing at all about Marxism, absolutely nothing—had formed a society with a political structure which was based on the economic relations of the country. The Marxists felt very confident of Marxism.

Today in the Russia of Stalin and Khrushchev, there are no longer Soviets. That is too dangerous. They vote as in ordinary countries. One man in his house, one vote. The vote based upon the position in the economic structure of society, that is gone.

So here, obviously, in the Soviet State was something new. It was new, but it was not final. We will come to that later.

## Europe after World War I

So there was Lenin and the Bolsheviks in a backward country. After the war and the revolution the production of backward Russia was down to 18 per cent of what it had been in 1914. They were waiting for the revolution in Western Europe to help them. Bourgeois society in Western Europe collapsed with the German Revolution in 1918 which brought the war to an end. Yet bourgeois society was able to recover. It recovered only to plunge us into the far deeper catastrophes of the last forty years.

There are certain things that I have not got the time—you have not got the time either—to go into now. I have one of my books here, *World Revolution*, in which I have accumulated a mass of the evidence of how bourgeois society was able to recover. The Second International of the workers saved it. They were the only people who could even keep order after the breakdown of society, particularly in Central Europe in 1918. This is not the opinion of observers. They themselves boasted about it. They don't boast now; they are not very proud of that now; but they boasted about it then. I have long extracts in my book here from Otto Bauer, one of the leaders, who says over and over again, "We were the ones who maintained bourgeois society in the Austro-Hungarian Empire." The Hapsburgs fled (I think one of them is now selling motor cars or aeroplanes or something). The German Kaiser, he went his way to Holland; the German generals were discredited. The war had been brought to an end by the revolution of soldiers and civilians against them, and the workers turned to their leaders of the Second International, the Social Democrats as they were called. The Social Democratic leaders struck down all those who were for the revolution and maintained bourgeois society. It is a horrible thing to read about today, especially when we see the mischief and the misery they have caused by propping up capitalism when it was on its knees. No force was in existence to stop them. If there is anybody here, or anybody here who knows somebody else who wants to come—I will be very satisfied to sit down when my time is finished and hear him say something different to this and give some evidence. I warn you, he will be systematically destroyed as soon as he is finished.

## Noske and Scheidemann

What happened after World War II in 1945 was that the Russian Army from one side and the American and British Armies from the other moved so fast that there was no opportunity for the masses of people in Europe to deal with those who had led them into the war and disaster. Or wherever they attempted it, they were stamped upon, especially by the Russians. But in 1918 the armies were not there. The armies had not reached Berlin and the rest of the cities. All of them were still under the German control and the moment the German Army was defeated, and the German rulers and many who were concerned with the war fled or hid, the whole situation was open. Lenin told the Social Democrats that all of the resources of the Russian State, the Russian Army and the people of Russia were at their disposal. He begged them to make a revolution, to create a socialist society. He said that Russia was not in front but, backward as Russia was, if Germany made the revolution, Russia would once more be behind, and Germany would once more lead Europe. They refused. My friends, look at Europe today; look at what Germany went through under Hitler from 1933 to 1945; think of the waste of World War II. Look at Germany, cut in two. Look at Berlin. If they had established the socialist society in 1919 as they were perfectly able to do, look at the millions of lives and the vast quantity of labor and production and effort that would have been saved. There was no problem to take it over, but they refused.

The men whom you should study—I can only mention their names—are Noske and Scheidemann in Germany, and Otto Bauer in Austria, Vienna. Noske and Scheidemann were so determined to preserve bourgeois society that already in 1919 they were intriguing with the German generals to establish a republic and the German generals were to support Noske, the Social Democratic leader, as President. Those German generals who, with the Kaiser, had led them into that mess for four years; the Second International preferred to go with them rather than with Lenin and the revolutionary elements in Germany.

By 1923 the revolutionary upsurge was over because people, as Trotsky has pointed out, are not by nature revolutionary. A revolution takes place because people are so conservative; they wait and wait and wait and try every mortal thing until they reach a stage where it is absolutely impossible to go on and then they come out into the streets, and clear up in a few years the disorder of centuries. By 1923 the thing had quieted down, but something new then appeared in Europe—Fascism. In 1919 it came with Mussolini in Italy, and in 1922 Mussolini made the famous "March to Rome"; Mussolini himself marched sitting in a railway train.

## Fascism Appears

Now you must understand that up to 1917 the idea of a socialist society, a Workers' State—that was considered a lot of nonsense. But after 1917 there was the thing itself in Russia, and in addition, Russia formed this Communist International. European capitalism, European landlords looked at this and took a new look at parliamentary democracy. You couldn't depend on the Age of Reason and all that anymore. (Rousseau was coming into his own now.) Now, the working class movement, as Marx always insisted, its great strength was that it did not have to organize itself. In an advanced industrial society capitalism organizes the working class by putting them together in huge factories, by putting them all to live in the most convenient spots to get to work early in the morning. So that Marx's essential point is that the working class is united, it is disciplined and it is organized by the very mechanism of capitalist production itself; and he says the more progressive capitalist production is, the more it unites those who are destined to be its grave-diggers: Marx is a wonderful writer apart from anything else. But other persons besides Marx were looking and seeing, and they said, "Well, we can't organize in a factory but we will organize outside." And Mussolini formed the Black Shirt Movement. The Black Shirt Movement of Mussolini and the Brown Shirt Movement of Hitler were organized for the sole purpose of destroying the threat of a socialist society that the working class now posed, with the example of a Soviet state actually in existence. They built battalions of dissatisfied middle class elements, and thugs. There is nothing else to it—at least there is plenty, but nothing that really matters. Mussolini's program was universal suffrage; everybody to have the vote; women to have the vote. They did not have it in Italy; up to 1945 they did not have it in France. In 1919 Mussolini said: Fascism—progress; women must have the vote; sick benefits, sickness insurance, old age pensions. Mussolini's Fascist program. Confiscation of profits by income tax up to eighty-five per cent. War profits, total confiscation. The wealth of the clergy—the Roman Catholic Church for various historical reasons is extremely wealthy in Italy—confiscation of the wealth of the Catholic Church. The socialists were attacking the idea of a standing army—Mussolini proposed abolition of the standing army. Instead, a workers' militia—arm the whole population so that in case of war everybody defends the country and you have no army to attack the workers. That was Mussolini's Fascist program.

Now that teaches us one thing: that even this, the most desperate reaction that Europe has ever known could make an appeal to the middle classes only on the basis of what could pass as the initial stages of a socialist program. But what Mussolini, and later Hitler, made clear to everybody was: this is my program, but the only way we can get it is by crushing the Marxists, i.e., the proletariat. The middle classes, fed up with the Second International, and seeing the workers split in two, went with Mussolini. Europe was in turmoil. People had been rooted out of their traditional status and the middle classes went with Mussolini, the Social Democrats would not fight and the Communists could not fight.

## The Name of Hitler's Party

Fascism came into power in Europe and Europe was plunged into the ruin and degradation of 1933 to 1945. Hitler, the Fascist, was able to come to power and destroy Europe between the quarrels of the Social Democrats and the Communists, the Second International and the Third International. Between them they had about 75 per cent of most of the large towns in Germany, and a larger majority of the population in voting than Hitler then had. But they fought one another, the Communists in particular, with more bitterness than they fought him. It is obvious today that by this failure these two organizations had proved that they were unfit for any proletarian or socialist purpose. More of that later.

Of Hitler's program, I have nothing to say. I will tell you only the name of Hitler's party. I wonder how many of you know it; it is one of the great facts of European history. If you know that, you know much about modern Europe, particularly Europe today. The National Socialist Workers Party of Germany. That is the name of Hitler's party. That is the name of the party that destroyed the German working class movement and tore to pieces every element of rationalism and parliamentary democracy in Europe—the National Socialist Workers Party of Germany. He could not dare to come forward in Germany, even with the obvious intention of destroying the Marxist movement, without saying, "I am for socialism too and I am for the workers." That is the situation; that was the situation in Europe yesterday and it is still the situation in Europe today.

How did Hitler come to power? Now the movement of history begins to get completely international. What happened in Germany is only to be understood if you take a look at Stalinism in Russia. Nowadays and from those days there is no history of any single country anymore.

That's over. The Bolsheviks and Lenin held on til 1923, and then two events took place of great importance in the history of Russia. Number one, Lenin died; and number two, the German Revolution tried again in 1923. It failed, and it was clear that this Socialist European Revolution that the Russians were depending upon for the salvation of their immature socialist state was not coming, would not come for some time. What was to be done? A tremendous struggle broke out and Stalin finally won; and for this evening's purpose I will summarize Stalinism in three points.

## Stalinism

Number one: the destruction of the Leninist Bolshevik Party. This is not a phrase nor a symbol. He destroyed it completely, root and branch, materially and spiritually. Trotsky was exiled, and was finally murdered by a Stalinist in Mexico. Zinoviev, Kamenev, and the great leaders of the Russian Revolution—the founders of, in my opinion, up to 1923, the greatest political party the world has ever known—they were dragged up in trials before the public, confessed to all sorts of unimaginable crimes, and then were ruthlessly executed within twenty-four hours of their condemnation. Today any book published by the Russians will tell you that Trotsky, Zinoviev, Kamenev, Bukharin and various other names that I do not want to go into, were not only traitors after the Russian Revolution, but from the very days that they joined the Communist Party had acted in the Communist Party and helped to overthrow bourgeois society in Russia as agents paid and carrying out the instructions of the imperialism of France, Britain and the United States. That is the history that is taught in Russia up to this day. Any Russian history book—there are usually some about—will tell you that that is the history of the Russian Revolution. So that they were not only murdered, sent to Siberia, put into prison, sent to convict camps, etc., but finally executed. Stalin took pains to destroy their very memory and particularly what they stood for, in the minds of the Russian people. When people say that Stalinism is the same as Leninism, it is very strange that Stalinism could only establish itself in power by the complete physical and spiritual destruction of everything that the Bolshevik Party stood for.

Having eliminated rivals and established its own power at home, the second thing that you must note about Stalinism is its complete repudiation of the revolution by the Stalinist parties abroad. Lenin had organized the Third International on the strict lines on which he had organized his pre-war Bolshevik Party. After Lenin's death, this degenerated into a bureaucratic subservience to Moscow which continues to this day. The Stalinist-controlled parties have never made a revolution anywhere. Where they have taken power in Czechoslovakia and Rumania and Hungary, etc., the Red Army marched in front and they marched behind, but they do nothing. No one here, or no one whom you can bring, can give the slightest evidence of any revolution carried out by the Communist International under the direction of Moscow. One very great revolution has been carried out in the world by a so-called adherent of Moscow, and that is the Chinese Revolution of Mao Tse-Tung. But we know it today. You can read it in the various places. The best place to read it is in a book by Isaac Deutscher. Mao, that very sinuous Chinese, went to see Stalin and Stalin told him, "Don't you go and make any revolution in China. Don't. Go and make an arrangement with the Americans, Chiang Kai-Shek, and work out some coalition government for China," and Mao said, "Yes, absolutely." And then Mao went and led the revolution to success. When he was victorious he said, "Our glorious comrade Stalin is the one who has helped us to make this revolution. Long live Stalin!" Stalin absolutely opposed any revolutionary struggle for power by a Stalinist party. That is one of the causes of the destruction of the working class movement in Germany and the coming into power of Hitler. I hope that I am not wasting time when I point out that the coming into power of Hitler was not merely a question of the destruction of the Marxist movement. It was a question of the destruction of Western Europe. It was held together by the United States; otherwise it was finished.

## Stalinism and Hitler

In 1929–1930 Hitler had about 30 members in the German parliament. In 1929 comes the greatest of capitalist economic crises, the Great Depression; millions of unemployed in Germany. Elections in 1930. Hitler wins over 200 seats and at once it is clear that the Fascist movement is on the way. Hitler gets very powerful; he gets money from the big capitalists and reactionaries. He claims to be socialist and for the workers, but he says the first thing to do is to destroy the Marxists. All the capitalists agree that that kind of socialism and workers' party suits them very well. He built up his Brown Shirts and they walked about in their brown shirts and their big boots stamping all over the place.

By 1931–1932, the situation is becoming very acute and it is clear that the future of Germany and, with it, the future of Europe for many years, is going to be decided by who will win that battle—the working class movement on the one hand or Hitler's Brown Shirts on the other. The German Communists got instruction from Moscow to let Hitler come into power. These things are very difficult to say to an audience that is not familiar with the material and cannot go to town tomorrow morning and buy the books. I have brought here my own book written in 1937. I have 52 pages (the Chairman will corroborate) on Germany in those days, and the title of the chapter is, "After Hitler, Our Turn." That was the slogan of the German Communist Party in Germany from 1930–1931 right up to the time that Hitler came into power in 1933. Let him come in. He will be a failure, and then we will make the revolution. They were the specific instructions of Stalin.

Trotsky was in exile in Turkey at the time, and he gave the warning. I want to repeat a part of what he said, because in those days those notable liberals and democrats and publicists and writers in papers and defenders of democracy against the totalitarian—I would like to make a collection of what they had to say before Hitler came into power and after. I could tell you one of the most notorious statements of one of them—Mr. Lloyd George, that great democrat who had led the slaughter of so many millions of young men in order to defend democracy against German militarism in 1914 to 1918. He said, "Let Hitler come into power. When Hitler comes into power we should not attack him, because he forms a barrier against Russian Communism." Mr. David Lloyd George, defender of democracy between 1914 and 1918, leader of the war to end wars. I know these birds, you know, and inside here, in Mr. Comma's Academy of Learning, I exercise—and I hope I shall continue to exercise—a certain moderation; but I can assure you I do it not without effort, and I am looking forward to the time when I shall be able once more to stand up and speak to people who would not expect me to be moderate in speaking about these crimes.

You see, they encouraged Hitler, most of them. Haven't you read Mr. Churchill's book in which he says that World War II was a totally unnecessary war? There must be some people here who have read that. It is the beginning of his book on World War II; he says the war was totally unnecessary, and it was. They could have stopped Hitler before. They said, "No, no. He is going to suppress the Communists, and that is going to save us." Anyway, let us preserve the academic tone and tempo.

## Trotsky and Naziism

Trotsky was in Turkey. I remember very well the pamphlets that he used to write at the time. The German Communists had given out the slogan, "Don't fight. Let Hitler come into power. After Hitler our turn." And Trotsky wrote a passage which I will never forget. I no longer can support his doctrines and I have opposed and will oppose what he stands for with all that I have. I believe it is dangerous. But nothing can make me and people of my persuasion forget the grandeur of his leadership of the Russian Revolution, his command of the armies of Russia in the Civil War, and what he did to warn people as to what was going to be the result of the coming into power of Hitler in Germany. All the great leaders in the Foreign Offices and the great prime ministers and the rest of them knew nothing; if any of them did, they said nothing. They sat down and watched. Mr. Churchill gained his great reputation because he was one of those who constantly shouted, "That man is dangerous!" The others said, "He is a bit unpleasant, but we have to keep a balance."

Trotsky, however, wrote somewhat as follows (I am quoting from memory): "The coming into power of the National Socialist Party will mean the extermination of the flower of the German proletariat, the destruction of its organizations and the destruction of its belief in itself and in its own future." He went on to say that when you noted the sharp capitalist contradictions in Germany as compared to what they were in Italy when Mussolini came into power, the hellish work of Italian Fascism against the Italian workers would be a pale shadow of what Hitler was going to do to the workers in Germany when he comes into power.

"Retreat, you say, you Communists who yesterday were talking about the immediate revolution. Leaders and institutions can retreat, individual persons can hide, but the working class will have no place to retreat to in the face of Fascism and nowhere to hide."

He continued: "If the monstrous and the improbable were to happen and the Communist Party were to refuse to take the field against Hitler now, what will happen is that the bloody extermination of the vanguard of the German proletariat will take place after the seizure of power by the Fascists and not before. Disrupted by the destruction of its organizations, disappointed in its leadership, the struggles of the German proletariat against Fascism after Hitler comes into power will be nothing but a series of futile and bloody convulsions.

"Ten proletarian insurrections, one after the other, ten successive defeats will not so much demoralize the German proletariat as if now you counsel it to retreat, and it does not fight, when the question is posed, 'Who is to be master in the German household?'"

The Communists continued with their slogan: "After Hitler, Our Turn." So it was that he came into power. He never had a majority of the German people. He led no revolutionary struggle like Cromwell or Robespierre or Lenin. He used to talk about "heads will roll" but his Brown Shirts of middle class young men and thugs fought no serious battles.

## The Proletariat and the Middle Classes

I intend no offense against school teachers and clerks and bookkeepers, etc. They could wear shirts of whatever color they like—they cannot in fighting deal with the proletariat of an advanced country. When ten thousand school teachers, bookkeepers, the writers and talkers like myself, and editors and so forth, vote, that is ten thousand votes; and they can have one thousand extra and have eleven thousand votes and defeat ten thousand workers, in votes. But the moment a revolutionary struggle is on, the workers—this group takes the railway, the other one the waterfront, the other one turns off the electricity, and the other one stops the transport; the teachers, etc., can only make some noise but they cannot do anything; they can send the children back home or bring them back or something. (laughter) In all struggles of this kind it is the proletariat that is master of the situation. The moment any government breaks down, then they can take charge. But these two Internationals crippled and hamstrung the workers of Germany. Hitler destroyed both of them; smashed their movement to bits; executed the leaders. He used to execute them with an axe, cut off their heads; let the blood flow; let everybody see. And when he was finished with the proletariat, he turned to the liberals and the rest of them who had stood aside and allowed this to take place. He finished up with them too. It is from there Europe moved into the war. The barrier against the war was the German proletariat to stop Hitler. Don't forget that. The others could stop him afterwards at the cost of untold destruction and the death of God knows how many millions of men. But he could have been stopped by the German proletariat before he had done anything; and the German Communist Party took the position it did under the instructions of Moscow. Stalin did not wish to be disturbed with any revolution. He believed that it would only make a lot of trouble for him.

## Stalinism Destroys Bolshevism

The third point is a positive point in regard to Stalinism: First he had to destroy the Party. Instead of the proletariat he put the bureaucrats in power. Then very late and after opposing the idea, he said, "I am going to lay the foundations of a modern industry in Russia." The German Communist Party and the other Communist Parties he saw as organizations that were to keep up activity and so forth outside, so as to keep the imperialists away from him. He did not know the defeat of the German proletariat meant inevitably the attack upon Russia by Hitler, but he laid the foundations of a modern industry in Russia. There is no question about that. Whether the methods and the circumstances under which that foundation was laid are, even today, justifiable, is a matter which is debatable. For myself and certain of my comrades and others, we opposed it all through; not it, but him. It cost the lives of perhaps seven to ten million peasants in the collectivization. Russia became undoubtedly the most barbarous modern state Europe has ever known. Some ten per cent of the economy was produced by "convict" settlements, under the control of the secret police, in places where it was difficult to carry machinery and so forth. Millions of people were working there. They dug canals and mines, just as in the old Greek and Roman days; and that came to an end not because the Russians stopped it or when Stalin died—or, as I believe, was murdered. It was stopped because of the tremendous strike that took place after the last war when it became clear that they could not hold the prisoners there any longer. The bureaucratic mismanagement, the brutality, the murders, judicial and injudicial—they would fill twenty volumes. I cannot ever accept that a whole generation should be sacrificed for future generations. One of the consequences you have seen in Communist policy in Germany. Such a method of production put an end to the aims and ideas of Marx and Lenin, both outside and inside Russia. The consequences will be with us for a long time.

Why then do I say it is debatable? In this sense. There are a lot of people who say, "You see the cruelties, you see how awful that is, your Workers' State." Pay no attention to them. They have a little position for themselves somewhere and they are defending that. Let them explain the history of capitalism during the last fifty years. One worldwide disaster after another, and no end in sight. No. There are Marxists, however, who say: "Marxism teaches that production is the basis of society; it is obvious that Russia, from being one of the most backward countries in Europe, has now become a country which is able to challenge the United States" (and rob a whole lot of other countries of their power and add it to hers, which is not necessary but also is part of power). Stalinism did this and they accept it. I, for various reasons, some of which I have explained, have been and am still opposed, not to what he did but the methods by which he carried it out. Others have different opinions. I have to leave it at that for now.

## A Note on Trotskyism

Now I have to say a few words about Trotskyism. Whereas many of us denied that Stalin's Russia was a Workers' State, Trotsky and the Trotskyites have always insisted that it is. They say that as long as the property is nationalized, you can plan production and this makes it socialist. We say that as long as the working class is not managing production, all that you have is capitalism in a new form—state capitalism.

## The United States

Now for the United States in this period.

The great problem of the United States in the modern world is: will it in time develop a proletarian movement and a proletarian party as the other countries in Europe and Asia and Latin America have done? The great problem of the United States, with all due respect to the color of the majority of my audience, is not the Negro Question. (If this question of the workers' independent political organization were solved the Negro Question would be solved. As long as this is not solved the Negro Question will never be solved.) Is the U.S. going to develop a proletarian party, Social Democratic or Communist or both, as Britain, France, Germany, Holland, China, Ceylon, Burma, India, Brazil and all the rest have done? Is the United States destined to be the solitary exception to the universal law that Marxists proclaim and other countries have followed? That is the question. Because the day that the United States established a proletarian party, whatever its program, the whole world situation would be at once changed. At present the American proletariat looks this way, at the Democrats, and sometimes that way, at the Republicans; these American capitalist parties go round and round all the time. The common talk is that the United States, owing to its wealth, creates a bourgeois life for its workers and they will never join a definitely proletarian party. Let them explain why these workers, despite all the economic advantages claimed for them, only recently staged the steel strike, one of the greatest of modern times. As has been said on so many occasions: we shall see.

Meanwhile, a few words about what happened to this powerful capitalist economy, this country where the workers were, are, and will ever be so rich that they will never form a workers' party. When the Great Depression hit the United States in 1929, it hit harder in this most advanced capitalist country than it did in any other country in the world. The official statistics will tell you that there were about twelve or fifteen million unemployed. I have been assured—and if I had the time I could prove it—there were nearly twenty million people unemployed in the United States between 1929 and 1932. The country was helpless before the capitalist crisis and more helpless than most of the others because it had not expected this. Here is where Roosevelt came in. Mr. Roosevelt, by means of sanctioning and encouraging trade union organization, social security, the rights of the working class, old age benefits, workmen's compensation, disciplining the banks, etc., was to bring the United States—up til then the apostle of an unlimited free enterprise—into line with what had taken place in the other countries of Western Europe. He did this without forming a proletarian party. That was the great contribution of Roosevelt to American capitalism, others will say to American democracy. It was a tremendous political feat, and Mr. Roosevelt and his wife together have a place in American history and the minds of the American people which will never be forgotten. Before Roosevelt and the New Deal, free enterprise and independent action by yourself for everything reigned as the unchallenged ideology of the United States. When Roosevelt was finished, that was finished. The government was now held responsible for those who were in difficulties owing to the difficulties of a capitalist society. In most of the countries of Western Europe, this had been carried out directly or indirectly by proletarian or labor parties of one kind or another. Roosevelt carried it out in the United States through the Democratic Party.

This Democratic Party consisted of the advanced elements, proletarian and liberals in the North and West, and the Southern Bourbons in the United States, who maintained a social regime of the most oppressive kind, feudal in many aspects.

## Roosevelt Wanted a New Party

In 1944, Mr. Chairman, President Roosevelt—the greatest political leader of the United States of the twentieth century (present company excepted; I do not want to say anything against General Eisenhower)—Roosevelt wrote a letter to Wendell Willkie, the leader of the Republican Party. (You will find the letter in Judge Rosenman's book, *Working with Roosevelt*.) In that letter Roosevelt told Willkie what amounted to this: "I can do nothing more with these Southerners who are in the Democratic Party. You have a Liberal wing in the Republican Party. Split them away from the Republicans, and bring your Liberal wing and Republican youth to me. I will chase the Southerners out of the Democratic Party. You and I will join together and we will form a genuine Liberty Party in the United States. I will run as President, and you will run as Vice President; and in 1948 I will retire and you will take over." Willkie told him, "O.K., I will." Willkie, however, lost in the primaries and Roosevelt died a little while after. But it is important to note (all this Nixon and—what is the other one's name? Kennedy? Kennedy-Nixon and Nixon-Kennedy, Kennedy-Nixon, Nixon-Kennedy business is insignificant compared with this): Roosevelt not before but after the New Deal said, "I have now reached a stage where I cannot go a step further as long as the Democratic Party is tied up with these Southerners." And he was ready to take the first step to form what he called a Liberal Party. He and Willkie may have formed it, and they would have called it a Liberal Party, but I do not think it would have remained Liberal very long. I am not exactly a young man and I am confident I am going to see—far less a lot of you, you are going to see it—that the United States will have to follow the political course that other capitalist countries have followed.

So there we are in 1939 with Hitler in power in Germany, moving to the war. The workers in other countries in Europe divided between Social Democrats and Communists, and the United States having just made a tremendous step forward but still under the aegis of capitalism—capitalist political parties. They all are moving to what I shall call the final crisis. (applause)

# Chapter Four
## Thursday, 18th August, 1960

MR. CHAIRMAN, LADIES AND GENTLEMEN:

Listening to the introductory statement about the singer who is to come—by Mr. Rogers—and remembering also the glimpse I had in the other room of her photograph, it struck me that it would be very helpful if that lady herself, or persons of equally exotic charm, could undertake to speak on Marxism as well as sing. The doctrine, then, would need not only its logic and convincing realism but it would be assisted also by what most people seem very happy to pay attention to. However, I must say, without making any reference at all to my exotic charm, but rather to my sweating up here and sweating before I came, that we seem to be going along at least with not too much opposition and a certain sympathy from the audience which is very helpful. It enables me to cover more ground than ordinarily.

Tonight, however, I propose to talk with you under the headings of "Atomic and Global Warfare," the "Passing of Colonialism," "The U.S.A. versus U.S.S.R.," "Immorality of Global Warfare" and "The Hungarian Revolution." I propose to take up certain aspects of modern civilization which are—I do not know, but by good luck the Chairman used the word—very explosive. Nevertheless, we are going to deal with them with a certain sense of realism; and tonight I am going to do something which I very rarely do, which I do not like to do, because it breaks the communication between the speaker and the audience. I am going to read right at the beginning a section from the *Times Literary Supplement*, June 28th, 1957. Now the *Times Literary Supplement*—I have a private name for it; I call it "Old Solemnity"—is a very serious, very sober magazine of the British ruling classes. The daily *Times* is already one of the great pundits of journalism. It is a very good newspaper, in its own way, for its own purpose. But the *Times Literary Supplement* appears only once a week,

and in it there are not very adventurous but very sober and penetrating
analyses of contemporary literature and contemporary society, which
have been more or less accepted by educated people in Britain. I want
that distinction to be clear.

The *Times Literary Supplement* claims that it is not in the vanguard.
It does not propose to say what is the latest thing. But whatever has
reached a certain stage of acceptance the *Times Literary Supplement* will
put it forward. I lay great stress on this and you will see why as soon as I
read the extract. The name of the article, front page, a full dress article,
is "Loyalties" and it begins:

"*A time of strained and breaking loyalties all over the world—in politics, nationalities, religions, moralities and families—is certainly a time
of troubles . . .*" There is a total breakdown in all the things that really
matter to civilization.

"*. . . Such a time has come upon us all, for the first time in history . . .*"
That is the age in which we live. We do not feel it so strongly out here,
although sensitive people do, but that is the situation in the civilization
of Western Europe and also in the East.

"*. . . That secular religion which once seemed the hope of half the
world—Communism—has equally become a prey to conflicts of loyalty,
nationalism and morality. In Russia, as in America, India and Britain—in
the Jewry of the diaspora and of Israel alike, as among dwellers in Arabia—
the old faiths cannot hold the young. Materialism rules the roost, and
societies bid fair to come apart at the seams. Worse, they begin to seem
unpatchable; yet no one knows, no one can foretell, what kind of society
will emerge as typical of the continental groupings (if not "the world State"
itself) towards which our familiar nation-states are being hustled.*"

Now that has been the main theme, the thesis of what I have been
talking about through these lectures, the consciousness of total breakdown—return to barbarism, the possibility of suicidal self-destruction;
and no way out—because those people have no way out, none at all. That
is what I have been talking about, and this evening I want to go further
into it. And I thought it would be just as well to preface what I had to
say with a clear statement of the decay, the degeneration, absence of any
political, social or moral standards by which the individual can guide
himself, which is characteristic of the world in which we live. I want you
to note that they mix together—India, Russia, the United States and so

forth. Naturally, in the *Times* every morning they would not speak like that, because they support the West against the East and democracy against totalitarianism and so on. That is what they have to do. But here they are very serious and the note of hopelessness is total.

## Hitler's Plan to Destroy Germany

I shall now go a little further, and I would like in advance to make it clear that I mean no offense to any nation or any race at all, but the truth must be told. In 1944 and in 1945 when the last war was coming to an end, Speer, who was in charge of German production, went to Hitler and told him that it was obvious that Germany was defeated and now certain steps should be taken in order that the population should not be reduced entirely to destitution. Hitler told him, "Destroy the waterways, destroy the gas works; destroy all means of communications and production; make Germany into a desert." Speer told him, "But even after we are defeated and peace has been declared, the population has got to live. We cannot reduce the country to this state." Hitler replied, "Those who are worth anything will die in the field of battle. The others who remain behind will be inferior and no consideration is due to them." The Fuehrer, the great leader of the German people, whose rise was to last one thousand years, was ready to destroy the country totally.

Now that is something new in history. Something new, particularly in modern history. On the other side of Europe, Joseph Stalin, during the previous decade, aiming at what he called "the collectivization of the peasantry," had taken a toll of something between seven and fourteen million lives. The figure is unknown. This much is certain, and students of population can easily verify it: when in 1939 the Russians held a census, the loss of population was so great and so shocking that the results of that census were never published and they had to take a new one.

I have spoken already of the concentration slave camps in the Arctic, far away in Siberia. Mr. Dollin has written an authentic book on that subject. How many millions we do not know exactly, but they were under the control of the secret police. Their production was about 10 per cent of Russian production, and the conditions and the morality could not be equaled in any other part of the world, except the concentration camps in Hitler Europe where, under German control, some six million Jews were systematically massacred. In many camps—we have records—so many per day into the gas chamber; done, ticked off, with all the care and scientific accuracy for which the Germans are famous. The brutality, the callousness and disregard not only for human life but for any moral standards and values, surpassed anything that I know in previous history.

## The Morgenthau Plan

Now I want to take that a little further, and here is where the trouble is going to begin. (Mr. Chairman, will you keep your eyes on those two pages for me, please.) The book is *The Struggle for Europe*, by Chester Wilmot. I was in New York somewhere about September 1944, and I remember when something called the Morgenthau Plan for Germany began to be talked about. The Morgenthau Plan proposed that Germany should be turned into a peasant country. All industries and industrial structures that were not destroyed should be taken away and the Ruhr, one of the great industrial concentrations of the world and the greatest industrial concentration in Europe, should be systematically destroyed and so treated that within the foreseeable future it could not possibly be reconstructed. Now I was a member of a political committee at the time, and when this piece of insanity began to be talked about, some members of the committee came and said, "Look at what they propose to do to Germany!" These comrades were working on a theory that human society was retrogressing, and they gave this prospect for Germany as a horrible example. I and one or two others said, "That is a lot of nonsense. They cannot do that. You cannot take a twentieth-century, industrialized country as Germany and turn it into a peasant country of the seventeenth century. You just cannot do it. Germany has twenty-five great towns of hundreds of thousands of people each. If you destroy all the industries, what are you going to do with the population? Not only the clothes and the conveniences of modern civilization, but the very food that people eat is dependent upon modern industry and their treatment in modern industry and their transport. You cannot take a population of some eighty million people, of whom over thirty million are working in industry and all that that involves in the rest of the population, and destroy the industry. What are you going to do with these people?" I dismissed the whole business—my friends and I—with contempt. We said, "That is a lot of nonsense. That is some sort of foolish propaganda."

It was not. The plan was sent up to Quebec for a meeting of President Roosevelt and Mr. Churchill (I think the date is the 15th of September) and they agreed to it. It is quite true that Mr. Cordell Hull and Mr. Henry Stimson opposed the plan, but with all their advisers at an international conference to decide what was to be the future of Europe after the war, Churchill and Roosevelt agreed to this destruction of one of the most highly civilized countries in Europe.

Now you have your opinions. I have mine. And when I speak about the barbarism, the degeneration and the decay of Western civilization, I do not separate East from West, and Fascism from Democracy. I take the whole as symptomatic of what is taking place today.

I could give you a lot more evidence but I want to stick to this particular episode. Goebbels, when he heard this, was transported with joy. For once he could carry on his propaganda by speaking the truth: no lies were necessary. Goebbels had been telling the German people that the Bolsheviks of Moscow and the Kremlin were plotting to destroy Germany from the East. Now he was able to say it was not only the Bolsheviks. The barbarians from Moscow and the barbarians from London and Washington were planning to do the same to Germany. "Look at the evidence," he said. "It is being printed everywhere, and their two great statesmen have agreed." The war was prolonged for many months by this, because the German people felt, well, where could they turn now? All thought of overthrowing Hitler or trying for some sort of peace, that was finished with, because of this monstrous declaration by the democracies. To follow what happened afterwards is very interesting—it illustrates the morality and the mentality of modern statesmen. General Eisenhower, leading the armies into Germany, discovered a stiffening in the resistance of the German soldiers. So he sent a message to Roosevelt, asking him if he couldn't do something about the proposal to destroy Germany. And on what ground? He said it was causing the progress of the army to be delayed. Anthony Eden, at another conference, said, "I am against this plan, absolutely against it. The Germans are going to be driven to starvation and we, the British, are going to have to feed them. I do not wish to be involved in this at all." The soldiers opposed it on military, the politicians on political grounds.

Goebbels was reveling in this propaganda gift, but Roosevelt could make no counter statement. Why? There was an election in the United States pretty soon—1944; this was September, the election was in November. Roosevelt said, "If after making that statement I now back down on it in any way, the Republicans are going to say, 'This man is weakening and is not carrying the war through as he should in order to come to early victory." He said it would have to stay til after the elections.

## Why Do They Behave This Way?

Now look at the bunch of them, please. Look at their attitudes to one of the most horrible political proposals that has ever been put forward, not only before a government, but before any public. I can assure you this is something new in the world.

Those of you who study history, when you read about a former dictator, Napoleon, you will find that the Duke of Wellington (round about 1815, when they had to decide what was to be done with France) and Metternich, that old scoundrel from Austria, and the rest of them, they were not like this. They had different standards. They had a different outlook. Their ideas of civilized behavior were in many respects crude, but it never approached this. At the end of World War I there was a stage of degeneration, but nothing like this. These standards by which we live today and by which our political leaders from the East or West, North or South, guide the destinies of the world are the lowest, most savage, most callous, most sadistic that I have ever seen or heard of in any kind of historical record.

You will understand, therefore, that in approaching this we have to come down to fundamentals in a sense beyond the ordinary. I don't know how people who support the politics which led to this will explain them. The habit today is to speak about original sin; they have gone back to Genesis. Man, they say, was born that way; he is evil. All the ideas of the nineteenth century about the progressive character of the development of human society they declare to be false. But whenever you hear someone talking about the natural evil in human kind, look out for hint: he will then say that the only way to keep order is by strong government and authority, of which he and his people, of course, would be the executors and organizers. That is where they are today—original sin. They believe that they are supported in this by modern psychology, the psychological studies of Jung and Freud. I am going to take those up later, but that is what we face. Add this to what I read at the beginning about the total breakdown in the minds of modern people, the absence of anything by which they can look forward to a harmonious, progressive and even a normal life in society. That is the world we are living in. I want now to give you some idea of what is the Marxist analysis of this state of affairs. We do not believe it to be a question of original sin. We do not believe that there is any inherent tendency to degeneration in modern man. We believe that by the very nature of capitalist society, its manner of development, it dominates the nature and character of politics and of human nature, and as it pursues its predestined course, it takes with it the men who are guiding it. In other words, in a capitalist society, in an advanced capitalist society, it is capital that rules, and it is capital that dictates the manners and morals of those who submit themselves to it.

Now I believe that that, at any rate, is a reasonable interpretation and allows us to look upon the prevailing barbarism with some sort of confidence, not only in human nature but in the development of a new state of society which will allow mankind to give rein and to develop those qualities and characteristics for which people have been struggling over the many centuries. To do this, to give you some idea of the movement of capitalist society, I shall have to go into some technical terms, but I do not think they will be beyond your immediate grasp. In any case, I am hoping that some of you will go further with some of these matters if you are not familiar with them already.

## Marx's Value Theory of Labor

The Marxist idea of the capitalist relation is a group of workers who have no property—neither land nor means of production—and who, therefore, are compelled to sell their labor to the man who owns, and now we have to add, who controls the means of production. One of Marx's fundamental theories is the labor theory of value, or, as it should be more correctly called, the value theory of labor. Marx says that in capitalist society the wage of the average worker is, classically speaking, what he needs for eating, drinking and shelter, and to reproduce his children so that future capitalists can have future workers. The law is not absolute.

In a very rich country, workers get a little more; a powerful trade union could get more than the minimum. But, he says, by and large, in dealing with theory you must take the absolutely pure situation from which you can work out variations. That is value production.

He says, now if, for instance, you are producing a motor car and you put one thousand dollars worth of plant into this type of car and then you put one thousand dollars worth of new material—rubber and steel and so forth—into that, that is two thousand dollars. And you pay your laborers one thousand dollars. He says nothing on earth can make you sell that for less than three thousand dollars. One capitalist can do that; on a national scale that is impossible. You cannot get less than you put in. Nevertheless, it is possible to get more than you put in. He says, when you purchase a laborer's work you pay him two dollars a day, but the work he does is not worth two dollars, it is worth two-fifty; and the sole source of profit at all times and in all types of capitalist production is the difference between what you pay the laborer and the value of the work that he puts into the product. He calls that the surplus value. What you put in in the way of plant and raw materials cannot produce any profit. He says, ten hundred pounds of steel put into a product will give you the value of ten hundred pounds of steel and nothing can ever improve that. But, he says, when a man *works*, that and that alone can improve the production. Pay him less than the value of his work, and you get the full value of his labor, and that makes profit—surplus value.

## Machines and Labor—Constant and Variable Capital

Now great battles have been fought over this theory. I have read many learned professors who try to explain it. They don't know what they are talking about, because they begin wrongly. You will remember we talked about Kant's Reason. Here we have another example of the same philosophical method. Marx's point of view is that you cannot prove the value theory of labor by itself. You can argue from now until 1997; you cannot prove it. He said the value of the theory is what it produces as you develop it, and if from the basis of your theory you get facts and ideas and movements which are an approximation to society as you see it, that is the proof of your original theory, and there is no other proof. So that on this basis of the value theory of labor, Marx says that capitalist production must be looked upon as dependent upon two forces—one, mechanized industry, and number two, labor. He gives these special names of his own. Constant capital he calls mechanized industry, and variable capital he calls labor.

I am not going to bother you with any detailed development of this, but Marx's idea is that as capitalism, on the basis of value production, produces and develops, the whole secret of it is that the constant capital, the quantity of industrial structure, of mechanized industry, increases in relation to the amount of variable capital, of human labor, which you have to use. A developed country is a country in which, for example, mechanized labor in relation to human labor is about 15 to 1. That is, say, in the United States—I am just giving illustrative figures—if in the United States mechanized labor in relation to human labor is 15 to 1, Great Britain, I expect, would be about 7 or 8, perhaps less, to 1. Russia would be about 4 to 1. As for Trinidad and Nigeria and similar places, they are none to 1 or something like that. (laughter) These of course are not real figures, but I give them to emphasize the enormous difference between a country like the United States and an underdeveloped country.

Now these numerical relations are of profound importance in regard to the development of capitalist society itself. Capitalism is a system that depends upon the world market. It is not a national system at all. If we look at the ordinary capitalist production, we can see one of the causes of its strength in the early days and one of the causes of its weakness today. If I have a factory and I am producing a motor car which costs me five thousand dollars, and the car, let us call it an "A" grade car—you know, one of those long ones you see in Trinidad from about here to over there (lecturer indicates)—I sell it for seven thousand dollars and all is well. It does not matter that this car I am producing is, as far as these monstrosities go, a good car. But suppose a man next door to me or in another country produces exactly the same car in every detail, but whereas mine cost me five thousand dollars to produce, his cost only four thousand. It is the nature of capitalist production that my factory is immediately useless. If he is going to produce for four thousand the same car I am producing for five thousand, nobody is going to buy my car, although it is exactly the same car. I may as well shut up shop, commit suicide, go in for something or other. This magnificent factory is automatically useless. Profit can be lowered, but two can play at that game.

## The World Market

Now it is not necessarily so in a socialist society or in any other society. My factory is still valuable: it produces a car just as good as any other one. But in the competition on the world market, the cheapest car is the one that will sell according to value, and mine must go. Capitalism has produced a great deal, but it has wasted quantities of production because of the necessity (the technical word: obsolescence) because of the necessity of getting rid of any productive mechanism which is not able to keep up with others in the market as a whole.

In the days of free competition that was the cause of the great progressiveness of capital, because periodically there would be a crisis. In this crisis people suffered. All those factories and production units which were not of the first class, which were not properly handled, fell apart. They would go bankrupt, and when the world market lifted itself out of the crisis, only the most advanced, the most highly productive elements, remained, and society would move forward from this higher level.

But at a certain stage capitalism begins to run to the government for salvation. Government also begins to enclose its production within the national boundaries because of war and tariffs. The capitalist, as soon as he gets into trouble, runs to the government and says, "Look how many people I am feeding, and look at the value of the production that I am producing for the benefit of the country. I am in a crisis. I am in difficulties owing to no fault of my own, but these miserable people in the other countries are under-selling me. They are paying their workers very little. Look how much I am paying mine. I would be glad if you could give me a subsidy of some kind." And as he has helped to put the government into power, the government looks into the matter and appoints a commission and tells the commission to examine the industry rigorously and give him the subsidy that he wants. He takes hold of the subsidy and, especially if an election is near, he goes to his political party, passes a little bit to them, and tells them to be careful to say how government interference is ruining capitalist production all over the world.

What exists in the world today in all these advanced economies is an absolutely artificial, non-competitive and therefore reactionary form of production. The free competition by which capital threw out what was not up to standard and passed on the advantages to the most advanced does not exist any longer. What we have today is state capitalism, and there is not much opportunity of backward industries being thrown out, because you must have full employment, and when the industries look as if there is going to be unemployment, particularly in countries like France and Britain, the government steps in and every effort is made to preserve it, whatever its value upon the world market. The United States, the most powerful of all, shelters behind tariffs. War preparations within national boundaries dominate production. In other words, even in theoretical terms, the special advantages which distinguished the system in its best days and which made it the most advanced system of production the world has ever known, those special advantages—essentially free competition—have been lost.

## Who Will Control the World Market?

That is the general theory. Now how does it apply to the world today? There are many people who believe that Russia, because private property has been abolished, is not subjected to the fundamental movement of capitalism. They are quite wrong. Capitalism—I cannot say it too often—functions on the world market. Today the competition is not for the selling of goods. The competition is for total control of the world market. What does global mean? Global war! What are they fighting for? I hope there is no one here who believes they are fighting for democracy versus totalitarianism or vice versa. It is for total control of the world market, and it is not a question so much nowadays of sale of goods. It is a question of the capacity to mobilize millions of men with great speed, to transport them with great rapidity and facility from one place to another; to be able to produce armaments of all kinds and what is required by an army at the greatest possible speed. It is to produce ballistics. It is to produce satellites. It is to produce one of these things that go in forty minutes from one end of the world to the other—missiles. That is what the production of the modern country is geared to do, to keep people going, but essentially to produce these. You produce these during the "cold" part of the war, and when you reach a certain stage and you begin to use them, that is the "hot" part of the war.

And now you see the consequences of mechanical development— Genghis Khan and Attila the Hun and these others committed many murders and massacres of hundreds and thousands of people; but they did not have atomic bombs. They just killed them, you know, with swords—struck them with a spear or something. You can do a great amount of damage with those but you cannot do too much.

But much of the problem today in this terrific struggle that is going on is that you begin with an ordinary atomic bomb; and the fellow over there has none. He, however, is working hard and he produces one a little better than yours, whereupon you produce one a little better than his, and so the competition which you carried on previously in regard to ordinary production has been transferred to the dominant armament industry. We have in full force the great principle of obsolescence whereby as soon as you have produced something, if the other country on the opposite side is able to produce it faster than you, no matter how many billions you have spent on it, you have to get rid of that and start afresh. They are at it all the time. So that the principle of capitalist production, which we have seen in previous stages of capitalism applied to the production of ordinary means of production and ordinary means of consumption, still governs the production of the most advanced sections of industry. That is the situation that we face—this constant development of industry along regular capitalistic lines for the mobilization of the population for the most advanced weapons of war and all the production which goes to the waging of national war by a national population. And with war after war, the killing of millions, the preparation in peace for ever more destructive weapons of war—this and not original sin breeds the mentality in which men plan and commit these most horrible crimes.

## The Domination of Capital over Men

Marx was very insistent that the mechanical development of capitalist production had a life of its own, and that it carried men along with it. They could not stop at any stage; the mechanical development automatically took them along as long as this infernal competition lasted; and therefore his analysis of the behavior of modern politicians and statesmen is, I believe, the most human, the most reasonable and the most hopeful, because it sees them as the victims of an economic system which has outlived its usefulness and in which the competitive elements, having been transferred from individual units of production to national states, now carry politicians, statesmen and people in a direction towards violent clashes which they cannot control.

I submit that that is perhaps—not perhaps—it is the only analysis that I know that can explain in reasonable human terms what is taking place and the threats of the destruction of the world and the suicidal interchange of bombs, atomic bombs, hydrogen bombs, etc. You look at them, at the people, and you wonder if the world, if men, have gone insane. They are in the grip of this economic movement, and although they are building guns and atomic bombs and hydrogen bombs and ballistic missiles, etc., the economic movement which is essential to capitalism is still continuing. It shapes the characters of the men who have to use them. Marx's analysis is that that is the movement on the one side. The opposite movement is the organization of labor in ever larger, more highly developed units. Only when these take control of industry will men control capital and capital will not control them. Labor will concern itself first with the development of men and not of capital, and only in this way will be broken the fanatical competition which threatens us with destruction.

## The National State

Now that is one example of where capitalism has reached today. I want to give you another example dealing with global and atomic war. If you study the history of capitalism you will see that it began with rather small units. These units steadily increased. (There was a certain amount of capitalism in Ancient Greece, you know. We know more about it during the last fifty years, and it was the capitalistic elements that caused the progressive developments in the City-States of Ancient Greece.) We watched capitalistic elements in the City-States of the Middle Ages, the immense comparative wealth that they produced; also the destruction that they caused in the civilization of the time because they fought each other to the finish—employers and workers and that stage of civilization were destroyed.

Now the stage which followed was peculiarly suited to capitalism, and under that stage capitalism developed splendidly. The political form suited to capitalism as we know it was the national state; the national state of Germany, of France, of Italy, of the United States, Canada and

various others; the national political state. Ancient Greece did not know
the national state; ancient Rome, though its empire covered the whole of
the known globe, did not know the national state. The City-States of the
Middle Ages were not national states. The national states are essentially
the states which were created and helped to create capitalism in the form
that we know it today. But we have to look at the modern world and keep
our eye on Western Europe in particular in the generation of modern
roads, modern motor cars and modern trucks, in the age of modern large
scale production. I remember in Detroit when at the River Rouge Plant,
there were, I think, one hundred and ten or one hundred and twenty
thousand workers working in the plant at the same time. Now you multi-
ply their families and those who have to feed them, to transport them and
the police to help to put them in jail when they need it, and so forth, you
have around this community of one hundred and ten thousand workers
in one plant in Detroit, you have a total community of some half a million.

## The Natural Unity of Europe

Now, with units of production of that size, you have rapidity of transport,
rapidity of communication, larger and larger urban units, greater and
greater interchange of different types of material, freedom in the use
of fuel, where formerly you had to produce near to coal and so forth
(oil is now rapidly transported), the telephone, radio communication,
television. It is clear that the units of production to which we were accustomed for many generations and which reached their greatest heights
in the old days, say, before World War I, are today outmoded. Europe
is crying for unification. These little countries with their customs barriers, each with its own cotton and steel and so forth—Belgium, Holland;
Belgium with its eleven million people, Holland with its nine million
or something of the kind; even France, Germany, Spain, Portugal—all
these. As for Hungary, Rumania, Bulgaria, Czechoslovakia and all of
those scraps of states—everybody knows that those today are an anachronism—not the people, not the language, not the national culture, but
the economic structure that each holds for itself. Europe is crying for
unification—production on a continental scale. And these wars that we
are seeing are not just wars for the sake of war. It is because substantial
sections of the European population in every country feel the need for

this unity. In one respect the Kaiser's attempt in 1918 was an attempt to unify Europe, under the domination, however, of one national state. That is the failure. Hitler's attempt to unify Europe was another attempt, a response to an obvious objective need. Today the democrats are trying. They have formed the European Common Market and they have the Coal and Steel Community. Nevertheless, they remain knitted within their national borders.

The problem is not only themselves knit within their national borders. The national state today is an anachronism and it in another way is one cause of the degradation of modern society. Great Britain as a national state must see to it that Europe does not unite. Isn't that a commonplace of British policy? What they call the balance of power? So that, you see, the national state becomes not only a barrier to the development of capitalism in the old way, but it now becomes a political barrier to the development of society. In addition the United States now cannot have any unification of Europe. The Atlantic is only a pond. The United States constantly backs Britain to maintain the balance of power on the continent of Europe. So that the world is moving economically and socially in a certain direction, but for the preservation of the interests of the national state, it is continually being torn apart by war; and when men find themselves in these retrogressive positions they are liable to take the steps and do the things that I began with at the beginning. The idea of destroying Germany—that inhuman, debased, degenerate program could only come to the minds of men for whom the preservation of their own national states took precedence not only over military but even social and moral values. That is the situation that they are in. The National State has to go or they will continue to behave as they do.

## Final Failure of the National State

Now a further example of the non-viability of the national state. The national state today, despite all its power and despite all the degradation to which it reduces the men who try to run it, never achieves its purpose. The British and the Americans sought to prevent the domination of Europe by Hitler in order to maintain the balance of power. What is the result? At the end of the war, Europe is closer to the domination of one power than it was when it began—before they spent all the men and money and wealth.

What is the situation of the Americans in the Far East, despite all the power? Their idea was to prevent the domination of China by Japan. If anybody was going to dominate China, they were going to dominate China. Not those backward Japanese whom they brought into modern life in 1850. They fought a tremendous war with what results? China today is dominated neither by Japan nor the United States. So that both in the West and in the East, in the objects for which the national states fought, they have failed, and they have failed because these objects in the modern world are unobtainable.

## The Road Out

Now what is the road out? The road out is a *continentalization*, to begin with, of the various economies. Europe must become one unit; but it is obvious that this unification—which even the national capitalistic states are trying to achieve—cannot be achieved by them. Marxists believe that if it is to be achieved, it is to be achieved by a new social class which is not governed by the political and social privileges and traditional interests of the national states which are three or four hundred years old. We believe that it can only be achieved by a social class which, from its very position in industry and the structure of society, can reach out to others of the same class in other countries. Mankind must leave behind the outmoded bourgeois class and all the obstacles which the national state now places in the way of an international socialist order. *THAT IS MARXISM.* It says: no longer the national political state but an international social order.

There are a lot of people running around busily building what they call a world state. They propose to join up Khrushchev, President Eisenhower and that very tall man, General de Gaulle, and Mr. Macmillan and the President of Brazil. They are going to join them all up in a world state. These people are very mischievous; they take important words and phrases, throw them around and make them look nonsensical. The capitalist system of production, the bourgeois national state under which capitalism grew to maturity, are today outmoded. The social order of the future is an international socialist order with classes in command or controlling the direction of the economy and political life who have got rid of the nationalist ideas, the nationalist policies and the nationalist economics of the bourgeois national state. The Russian Communists now put themselves forward as the force to unite Europe. That is one great part of their appeal. Their method is the same as Hitler's: force, brutality, suppression of freedom. They can only think in terms of a Russian-dominated Europe. The Socialist United States of Europe will be a free federation. The working class of Europe, in the three Internationals, shows that internationalism is inherent in it.

That is the Marxist position. I do not know of any other position. There is a position that is being preached now, at least they were preaching it up to the summit or up to just before the summit took place. It is a password called "co-existence." The moment one state tells another state, "Now we shall be able to practice co-existence," that means they are in mortal conflict. You don't have to tell your neighbor next door that you and he must practice co-existence. You just live together. This insistence on co-existence shows what is wrong—that co-existence between these two competitors has the very slimmest possibility of lasting for any length of time. Well, they reached up to the Summit and just as they reached Khrushchev said, "I am insulted, so no co-existence unless you apologize; but if you apologize, I will continue the summit with you and we will co-exist." It is quite ridiculous, the whole business. There is no sense to it at all. What is much more serious is that every now and then Khrushchev says, "You are troubling me there in East Germany. You are sending some plane to spy. If you go on with this, I will wipe away Western Europe." And then the Commander-in-Chief of NATO says, "Boy, I tell you, I will wipe away all of you over there." That is the level that they have reached. They are continually threatening to destroy one another or at least that half of the world in which they do not live.

So you see why it is that not only in vital economic relations but in equally vital political relations, Marxists base their hope for the future upon the working class. It is because the rulers of society, capitalists or state-capitalists, have dragged society down into the dreadful mess and ruin that it is in, and show no signs of policy or ability to get it out again.

So I have given you some idea—that is the best I can do—of why the capitalist system as it is today has outlived the conditions under which it was powerful and progressive, and it has outlived the particular political form under which it grew to maturity. The preservation of the national state leads to continual warfare for the maintenance of the balance of power, and, furthermore—this is its absolute condemnation—the aims for which the national state fights are today impossible of achievement. I cannot see how it is possible to make a greater condemnation. Today the national state has reached the stage where—and this is part of the demoralization of which I spoke—defeat will be a disaster, but victory also would be a disaster. What would victory today in a war between these national states mean? Nobody has any perspective that victory would mean anything. And that is the condition in which the world is at the present time.

## Mr. Macmillan and India

I expect some of you are getting ready to lean back and luxuriate in my remarks on the passing of colonialism. I want to make only a few remarks about the passing of colonialism and then go on to the Hungarian Revolution. The remarks I have to make about the passing of colonialism are three. (Some of the things I say I choose because I think they are easy for you to remember.) It is good to have certain key points in your mind at all times. This is No. 1.

Mr. Macmillan paid a visit to India after India was independent. The British ruled India for over three hundred years, but no prime minister had ever gone there. He was too busy drawing the profits and spending them for his country, but when the Indians became independent and Britain wanted them to remain in the commonwealth, Mr. Macmillan paid a visit to India. There he said something which is of great importance to me in particular, because it is the first time for many years that a British prime minister had said something with which I am in total agreement. That matters only to me of course. He said something like this: "The British stay in India cannot be appraised—no conclusion can be arrived at now. Future times will tell."

That is very important for us, because imperialism, even when it goes, is always just below the surface, and the tendency is to say that Indians, maybe they were a bit exploited, but look on the other hand what the British have brought to them. They gave them education. They gave them railway trains. They gave them this, that and the other, and therefore, although they took, they gave. It is a ridiculous argument, and

Mr. Macmillan had the sense to abandon it. It is ridiculous because what it means is that a country with the past of India, having arrived at the year 1600, would have remained there, incapable of advancing towards Western civilization, unless the British had colonized them. That cannot be accepted at all. It would be an insult to India. Japan did it without imperialism. No, the argument is silly when it is not malicious.

## Bourgeois Breakdown and Colonial Independence

Point No. 2 is that these colonies and ex-colonies are getting their freedom today with the ease that they are getting it because of the breakdown of capitalist society. Let nobody believe that if they were as strong as they were in the days of old, all sorts of impudent little states like Cyprus and Malta and Trinidad and Jamaica and Ceylon and all of them would be allowed to say, "Freedom, independence, set a date," and all that. They would not have stood for that. My view is that the passing of colonialism is part of the general decay of capitalism, and part of the general decay is the disinclination of millions in imperialist countries to carry on any of these imperialistic adventures anymore. Millions of workers don't want to have any part of it. The most striking example of that is Indo-China. You know who fought the war of Indo-China? Not the French soldiers, not the French Army; volunteers and the French Foreign Legion, including many of Hitler's soldiers who had nothing to do in Germany and were prepared to go fighting and see what they could get out of it. That was the great French war in Indo-China. So that the rise of colonial independence is a part of the breakdown of the system of capitalism and the national bourgeois state.

Point No. 3 is highly significant for the future. The newly independent states are uncorrupted by the tremendous weight of tradition and practice and habit which now burden the national bourgeois states, whether they are ruled by Labor or Conservative parties. Today they are in the very vanguard of the progressive forces of modern society.

## New Perspectives

I want to take Ghana and in a few brief words tell you what are the policies of this little state of five or six million people. Ghana aims at a United

States of Africa, and Nkrumah is very serious about it. He says, "At any time we are prepared to give up completely the national sovereignty of Ghana, which we fought so hard to get, in the interest of a united Africa." There is no European statesman who could say that. If he wrote it down, when he stood up to read that he was going to give up national sovereignty, he would choke. He could not say it. (laughter) Ghana and Guinea say, "We have nothing to do with either East bloc or West bloc." They say, "We do not want any kind of military bases on African territory. We will oppose it whenever we can." Sékou Touré says, "Not only no military bases, but no kind of economic or political subjugation of any part of Africa to either of the blocs." They say, "We are going to train people. If anyone comes to Africa to test any bombs, as de Gaulle did, we are going to march on the installation and try to put an end to it by force."

Usually even when political parties say these things, when they get into power as governments they forget them. But these are governments that are saying them, and the Convention People's Party of Ghana has got a huge settlement where people from all parts of Africa who are fighting against imperialism and oppression can come and live and get some food to eat—because revolutionaries are sometimes very hungry and miserable. They are thin because they have been working too hard under hard conditions. They get food and rest and paper to write on and somewhere to print and money to go back to fight the imperialists in Africa. Nkrumah has invited all states that wish to oppose nuclear warfare to form a non-nuclear club and condemn nuclear warfare for the barbarism that it is.

India's policy is the same, and these countries go to the United Nations—Arabia, the Asians, Latin America, all these small countries—and they pester the lives out of the big ones whenever any imperialist question comes up to the vote. Now America bribes some and Russia bribes and terrifies others, but by and large some of them take the bribes and vote against them. (laughter) They say, "Thank you for the economic aid; we would like to have some more technical aid; but your behavior in Algeria is shocking, and you should not have done that in Guatemala, etc." They vote against colonialism.

Very soon we in the West Indies are going to have somebody there, and he will be speaking and he will be voting, and I hope he will be speaking and voting right, because if he does not he can look out for one enemy and that will be me. (laughter) So that the passing of colonialism, you see, is a sign of the weakness of the capitalist bourgeois state and at the same time it provides ammunition for the breakdown of these imperialist states which dominated them before. Nevertheless, there is no question about it: the basic opposition to imperialism must come from the proletariat of the advanced countries. As long as they remain under the physical and mental control of their nationalist leaders, the present situation will go on. Therefore, I want to say a few words about the Hungarian Revolution.

## The Hungarian Revolution

You know what the Hungarian Revolution signifies? You know what was its leading characteristic? Its leading characteristic was that political parties and trade union organizations had nothing whatever to do with it. It was established by Workers Councils in every factory and in every department of the national life. And after a week of it, the Hungarian intellectuals asked the Workers Councils to form a Workers Council Government.

Now you will remember last time we spoke about the Soviet. I have traced carefully with you the outbreak in 1848 when they did not know what they wanted; then the commune in 1871 when they formed a legislative and executive body in one (with nobody instructing them). From 1889 they formed the Second International; the Russian Soviet came, in which factories elected people into what was essentially a political body based, however, on economic relations—something entirely new. Nobody invented it; nobody told them; they just felt that that was what they wanted at the time. The Soviet was the latest, and you had in the Soviets the two parties, the Second International and the Third, contending for power. In my opinion, the Second International and the Third International, the Social Democrats (the Labor Party) and the Communists, passed out of history as useful political forms in Germany in 1933. I have described how both of them allowed Hitler to come into power when united they could have overthrown him without any difficulty. Political organizations which allowed this to happen have thereby proved their incapacity to handle the problems of the day. The coming into power of Hitler, owing to the divisions and incompetence of the

Communist Parties and the Social Democratic Party, was a catastrophe not only for them but for the whole world. It will be many years before we get rid of the consequences of that. I will take that up in later issues when I will go more into the psychological problems which these crises have placed upon us. The Spanish Revolution took the Soviets further, but political parties still fought for power in them and so ruined them. Now we find that in 1956 the Hungarian Revolution formed the Workers Council, no Soviet. And do you know what was the decision of these Workers Council in the Hungarian Revolution, one of the greatest revolutions in history? They said, "No Communist Party, no Social Democratic Party, no Catholic Party, no small peasant parties in our Workers Councils. All of these parties for all of these generations have been leading or trying to lead, and always the reaction has defeated us in the end. This is a Workers Council. Any man who works in this industry, in this factory or in this office is entitled to vote for a representative, but no party is going to be represented here."

That is the latest development. It means very little to these clumsy-headed barbarians who do not understand the movement of history, but as a Marxist I have tried to show you how the socialist movement has developed from 1848 and how stage by stage without a single writer or theorist or publicist instructing them in anything, the workers have constantly developed new and more advanced political and social forms until they have finally arrived at the Workers Council, based upon a man's employment in all forms of industry or office activity. You elect a representative upon the basis of the number of men in that particular section of the industry and that grouping is at once economic and political and a social form. For us, the Marxists, it is the ultimate form of modern political development.

## The Rejection of the Party

That is why my friends and I have broken with Trotskyism. Trotsky was trying to form a Fourth International based on Lenin's conception of the party. We said that Lenin's conception of the party was a great achievement for his time, but that today Leninist Bolshevism is dead. Workers in advanced countries, i.e., where the proletariat is large enough and strong enough to lead the nation, will only be misled and corrupted and hamstrung and defeated by parties of this kind. The proletariat, we said, had to discover new forms, as it had always done. We said this in 1951, and so when in 1956 the Hungarian workers not only developed Workers Councils to the highest pitch but rejected the struggle of parties in them, when we saw this and examined it, we felt that we were right and, what is more, gained added confidence for the future of society.

One point I must not omit here. The party, adapted to local conditions and basing itself upon a careful examination of both the Second and Third Internationals, is still valid for countries which are underdeveloped, that is to say, where industry and therefore the proletariat is not dominant. One proof of the continuing validity of the party in those areas is the victories that they are winning in country after country.

## The New Form of Organization

Now for the last word I will leave you with to tie together the points of this evening. The new form is a close and intimate relation of the ordinary man in his labor and on the basis of his labor creating a social and political form over which he has immediate and constant control. Politics is not carried out in some other room by politicians but in the factory itself. Time is taken off for the industrial and trade union and political life of the country. It is done in the actual place of labor or the office, so that political life is not taken away from the people. Now the thing that Rousseau was so savage against—this close and intimate political structure—corresponds to the tremendous scope of the international continental organization. Because without this, an international organization would mean that the average individual person would be utterly lost, more lost than he is today. So that, as society moves forward towards an international organization to get rid of the national political form—not the national language, nor the national customs, etc.—to get rid of the political form of the national state in the interest of larger organizations of a continental scope for handling industry on the broadest scale; at the same time we see that the class that we say has to do that has worked out for itself ways and means whereby it would be constantly and immediately in touch with the greatly increased expanse of economics and politics.

Of course there are a great number of questions that the Hungarian Revolution did not answer and could not answer. The Russians destroyed it before it had lasted a few days. But it made a remarkable beginning. The miracle is that it did so much in so short a time. It is when you are familiar with the stage by stage development of the past—I have tried hard to keep this before you—that you are able to see what the Hungarian Revolution signifies. I believe that that is the way society has to go, and if it does not go that way we will have what I began with—ordinary human beings behaving as demons and monsters in a manner that would have been unthinkable during five hundred years of European civilization.

Til next time. (applause)

# Chapter Five
## Monday, 22nd August, 1960

MR. CHAIRMAN, LADIES AND GENTLEMEN:

I would like to begin by reading what the last two lectures will deal with. I must tell you—and I think it is right that you should know—that this is undoubtedly the most difficult course in any theme of politics or similar matters that I have ever given. The reporters are taking it down; I am going over the texts and I have the opportunity of really seeing what I have been saying. (laughter) The effect is most surprising: we have been covering an astonishing range, and I see that, by and large, although the course is long—six miles—nearly everybody who started is keeping up. There are between five and six hundred people every lecture and over one-half are here for every session. It is very striking and very satisfactory. These last two sections are going to break some new ground. That is what we have been doing every time, and I may say that although I am sticking to the headings, the things I am talking about are not exactly the things that I planned at the beginning; but we have gone on and I think you are following, and those who do not follow everything will be able to get the text.

I want to read what remains. Lecture No. Five this evening is called "The Battle for Survival," and the sections are:

(a)  What Is the Good Life?
(b)  The Welfare State—Democratic and Totalitarian;
(c)  The Exploitation of Sex—I have changed that to the Exploitation of Women;
(d)  The Exploitation of Class; and
(e)  The Exploitation of Race.

Lecture No. Six we call "Where Do We Go From Here?"
(a)  How We See Ourselves: Rimbaud, Joyce, D.H. Lawrence, Proust, T.S. Eliot, Ezra Pound, Jean-Paul Sartre, Hemingway, William

Faulkner—a representative selection of the most gifted of modern writers.

In opposition to them, I pose

(b) "The Undying Vision": Chaplin—that is our friend Charlie, who is one of the greatest men of this century; D.W. Griffith, the American movie director; Eisenstein, the Russian movie director; and Picasso.

In regard to Picasso, I am going to talk about only one painting by him. My wife bought a reproduction in the United States. I could not get one which I would have liked to bring from England—a reproduction of his great painting, *Guernica*. However, Mr. Comma has it, and I think by next time you will be able to see it as you come in. It has a very close relation to what I am talking about during these last lectures.

To continue.

(c) Science and Industry: The Grandeur of Automation and the Folly of Satellites;

(d) Science and Man: the theories of Freud, substantially; a few words about him and Jung and the theory of the unconscious.

And, finally:

(e) The Political Alternatives: The Ascent of Man to Complete Humanity, or Degeneration into the Life of the Cave and the Jungle.

And I mean that. They are living in caves in Sweden already, and I am sure every modern country is building caves. They do not talk about these caves; they don't want to frighten us more than we are frightened already.

So that we come now to "The Battle for Survival" and "What Is the Good Life?"

## What Is the Good Life?

I do not propose to preach any sermons here. Please get that out of your minds entirely. I am speaking about the good life from the point of view of society. It is a difficult question and it is made more difficult by the follies and inanities of statesmen. Let us presume for the sake of charity that it is political necessity (their necessity) which makes them talk so much nonsense. For example, Mr. Butler, who is an able man at his own British politics, rebuilt the political perspectives of the Conservative Party after its defeat in 1945—a thing that Mr. Churchill could not possibly do; but Mr. Butler has told the people in Britain that in twenty-five years' time—a quarter of a century—the standard of living will be doubled. It is the kind of inanity that I want to warn you against, and I would be glad if, when you hear it, you really express yourself, not offensively, but with the necessary contempt and scorn. That statement is without meaning. This is 1960. Fifty years ago, 1910, I am sure that the amount of goods, the quantity of services that were at the disposal of the average worker in a particular country were more or less about half what they are today. You know that in your own lives: what your fathers and grandfathers lived by, the goods and services they had were small in comparison with what you have today. That is the situation in Europe and in Britain as a whole. Has that solved anything—the doubling of the standard of living, what you have at your disposal to use, the goods and services which are twice what they were fifty years ago? Has that solved any social or political problems? The social and political problems are today worse, more acute, than ever they were in 1910. But, you see, when he says in twenty-five years "we" will double the standard of living, he thinks that he will have doubled the number of votes for the Conservative Party, because, you see, his party, if left in power, will have been the one who will have done that for the workers. It is the kind of quantitative analysis, vulgar materialism—materialism of the most vulgar type—which makes absolute ruin of any attempt to form any sociological or social analysis of the development of society. People today are concerned with whether they will be able to live at all in twenty-five years' time.

## The City-State Once More

The average Greek must have lived on what I expect would be today about fifteen or twenty-five cents a day. The houses in which they lived were extremely simple; the territory of Greece was very unproductive— chiefly dried fish, olives and olive oil, dried fruits. The houses were notoriously commonplace—four or five rooms, somewhere in the back for servants. But when you walked out in the streets of Athens you could see Plato, Aristotle, Pericles, Socrates, Phidias, Aeschylus, Sophocles and many more of that stamp, all at the same time; and they were active in the daily life of the city.

The question, therefore, of what is the good life is not to be judged by quantity of goods. What I said at the beginning is the most important: that community between the individual and the state; the sense that he belongs to the state and the state belongs to him. Rousseau, if you remember, expressed it with great violence. He said, "Before we have any kind of government, we have agreed to meet together, to work together; and I take my liberty, which is mine, my property, and I give it to the government along with yours, so that when I obey that government I am in reality obeying myself." That, in my opinion, was the greatest strength of the City-State and the great strength of the Greek individual—the basis of a good life. It is hard for us to understand, but a Greek citizen could not conceive of his individuality apart from the *polis*, the City-State. It made no sense to him to think of it otherwise; and recently I have been reading a modern writer on the Greek City-State who says that even when there was no democracy—when there was an oligarchy (government of the rich) or monarchy (government of a king) or aristocracy (government of the nobles)—even under these diverse regimes, the Greek had it in his head that the state was his and that the state belonged to him and he belonged to the state. If you observe their temples and their statues, it was centuries before the Greek ever put up a statue away from a temple. He would not put a statue in the middle of the square out there. The temple represented the state; and in the niches of the temple he would put statues; but the idea of a statue, i.e., an individual, somewhere else away from the building which symbolizes the state was something utterly foreign to him.

There the good life for the individual citizen begins. Today we do not see much of that. We do not see that very much except in periods of revolution when people get together behind a program and leaders. It is very rarely the state, an actual government. Sometimes it is a political party, sometimes it is a leader; and then you get an example again of what Rousseau means when he says that if the minority has to obey the majority merely because it is a majority, that is not liberty, that is not freedom. It may sound fantastic; it is not at all. Rousseau is insisting that the majority must represent the general will, and even if the minority is hostile but the majority represents the general will and the political leader or a political party most obviously represents the general will, then the minority must obey the majority because the general will is being expressed. The general will is expressed when its political form makes the individual feel himself part of the community. A mere majority vote over a minority—Rousseau and Hegel and others make it clear that when you have to obey because they have the police (they put you in jail if you don't)—but strictly speaking, from a philosophical point of view—that is not democracy. That is not liberty. I grant you that this is not easy. You have to grapple with it and discuss it and work it out. (Think of your own recent history.) A minority, that is to say a group that finds itself in opposition, can submit itself and obey when it feels that the majority represents and is building a national community. This I must warn you is the philosophical approach. But without this you cannot understand politics. And what is philosophy today becomes reality tomorrow.

## The Conclusions of Hegel

I am not going into Hegel's philosophical methods and what constitutes the good life, the good citizen. I cannot do it; it is too much. It would need six lectures by itself. But I will give you his conclusions. They are stated in very profound philosophical form, but I think we can make a beginning, and I shall give you one or two examples.

Human society is an organism; and he says that contradiction, not harmonious increase or decrease, is the creative moving principle of history. There must be opposition, contradiction—not necessarily contradiction amounting to antagonism, but difference, obstacles to be overcome. Without that there is no movement, there is only stagnation and decay. That was why the Greek City-States moved so far and so fast, and that is my hope for the development of the West Indies too. Those states were so small that everybody had a grasp of what was going on. Nobody was backward; nobody was remote; nobody was far in the country; and people in the West Indies are even closer because we have methods of transport that bring us very rapidly together. It was within this narrow range that with great violence of conflict and so forth the Greek state leaped from social position to social position and made its marvelous discoveries and inventions. That is the moving force, the creative movement in historical development. That is the first point.

## Development through Self-Movement

Another point. All development takes place by means of self-movement, not organization or direction by external forces. It is within the organism itself, i.e., within the society, that there must be realized new motives, new possibilities. The citizen is alive when he feels that he himself in his own national community is overcoming difficulties. He has a sense of moving forward through the struggle of antagonisms or contradictions and difficulties within the society, not by fighting against external forces.

Let me stop for a moment and give you one sharp example of that. We as West Indians feel that in fighting for the return of Chaguaramas and for self-government against British imperialism and so forth, we are fighting real political struggles. In a sense that is true. When the British go and the Americans go and the British flag comes down and the West Indian flag goes up and all face one another—it is then you are going to see real politics. That is not to say that what has happened up to now is not real. It is very real, but it is preliminary. When all that is achieved, then the fundamental forces inside this country, as in every country, will begin to show themselves. In fact Lenin's doctrine was, "We do not want to have imperialism; we want to get the imperialists out in order to carry on this struggle inside, free from interference by all these people." If I may venture a prediction based on historical experience, the exhilaration based on successful anti-imperialist struggle rapidly declines and a far more solidly based new social movement begins.

## The Mastery of Wealth and Knowledge

Now we come to the tremendous jump that Hegel makes and that Marx and the others follow. *It is not the world of nature that faces modern man.* When Descartes, Copernicus, Bacon, the Royal Scientific Society of England, Spinoza and Hume and the rest of them, and early capitalism, early science, began, they were fighting to overcome nature and to learn to discipline nature and to turn nature to the uses of men. That was the struggle for the beginning of the modern world. But not today. Today man has not conquered nature in general (you will never be able to conquer nature), but he is able to bend it, substantial qualities of it, to his own purposes; and the problem in the world today is not what it was for many centuries. You remember our friend St. John said there must be no sea because to cross the sea with their small boats was very troublesome and dangerous; also fruit trees would not bear once a year, but every month. You understand what he was driving at. The problem for centuries was to master nature. Not so today. The problem in the eyes of Hegel and in the eyes of Marx is the mass of accumulated wealth and scientific knowledge which man has built out of nature. That is the problem. It is difficult to see in the West Indies and in underdeveloped countries because we are still struggling to get some potatoes and to catch some fish and so on. But in the modern world today that is not the problem. In ten or twenty years it would be possible to feed adequately the whole population in the world. That will be no problem. The problem is how to handle, how to master the mass of accumulated wealth, the mass of accumulated scientific knowledge which exist in the world today. That knowledge is driving us to world suicide. Capital, I repeat, controls us. We do not control it.

This is so important that it is worthwhile going it over once more. Capital controls man. Man does not control capital. And this has reached such a stage that the great masses of men live in fear and anxiety. The good life for a modern citizen is impossible. We feel it here, but it is the great centers of population and industry that feel it most, and every human being is affected far more than he is consciously aware of.

## The Capital Relation

Let us look at the movement of capitalist production again. You remember my analysis of a national economy as being 15 to 1, capital to labor; 8 to 1; 3 to 1, etc. You remember too it is the competition to improve this ratio which is the driving force of capital. The Trotskyists say Russia is a workers state because private capital is eliminated. We say that private capital or no private capital, this murderous competition goes on. Russia cannot ever stop to use its advance for the benefit of the people. That is subsidiary. It has to get rid of a perfectly valuable plant, etc., to keep up with America, and vice versa. And until we have international socialism that will go on. The mass of accumulated wealth, knowledge, science— constantly preparing the basis for new weapons, new organization of industry, new processes—prevent men ever being able to stop. They have no choice. The good life for the citizen is under these circumstances impossible, even when he has enough to eat. Capital, the capital relation, is the relation of men who have nothing to sell but their labor-power, and men who control or own the means of production. It was not always so. In the best periods of the Middle Ages, for example, the peasant owned his land; the workman, the artisan, owned his tools. They controlled and ordered their own activity. It is interesting to note that England in those days was known as "Merrie England." Nobody would call the English today merry. Capital, you see, can transform national character.

The solution; Marxists say, is to put all this wealth under the control of the men who work in it. Then, and only then, will the mass of accumulated wealth and scientific knowledge be used for the benefit of the great mass of mankind. Otherwise you have value production. As long as the wealth and knowledge are being guided by people who are concerned with preserving their position and their managerial status, this fanatical competition will continue, and man will constantly produce more means of production, and constantly improve means of production; and now they have become means of destruction pure and simple.

I hope nobody believes that they really want to spend weekends on the moon. They are not really interested in that. You saw the other day that a satellite has been brought down in Russia with two dogs in it. Everybody is talking about the dogs; that is not in the slightest degree important. What is important is that it was brought down in a particular spot. They are frantically trying in Russia to have this thing going round and round so as to be able to bring it down when they please at a particular spot that they please; and you do not have to know too much geography to know which is the spot they wish to bring it down at. (laughter) But in the United States they are busy morning, noon and night with exactly the same; and it will not be very long—in fact I do not know if it is not happening already, that we will be living an existence in which these two will have these things going round and round; and the next thing now is not to have yours going round and to bring it down where you want, but to prevent his, to stop it and bring it down back where it came from. (laughter) That is where we are. And you get the fundamental point that Hegel makes and Marx follows. He says, "It is not the struggle with nature; it is not a struggle for good; it is not the struggle to overcome barriers, the seas, the rivers; or to produce power or heat." They say that is not the problem anymore. The real problem is to control this mass of machinery and scientific knowledge which is running away with us. I have indicated the Marxist solution. What other is there? I know of none. Our rulers of the great and dominant states are bankrupt, with no perspective but war and destruction. Is that so or not?

## The Pursuit of Happiness

What is the good life? An individual life cannot be comfortable and easy or creative unless it is in harmony to some degree with the society in which it lives. The individual must have a sense of community with the state. That is where we began. And that today is impossible. We tend to think of the good life in terms of individual well-being, personal progress, health, love, family life, success, physical and spiritual fulfillment. The whole point is that far more than we are consciously aware of, these are matters of our relation to society.

I am not saying that the individual human being is consciously striving to adjust himself to society. Not at all. Since the days of Aristotle and even long before, the philosophers have understood that man seeks happiness and seeks to avoid misery. It is as simple as that. Only that is not at all an easy thing in a complicated world. The thing to understand is that progress is not simply the increased use of goods. That is utility—utilitarianism. That was the doctrine essentially of the men of the eighteenth century. But progress is the incorporation into the social and individual personality of the stage that society as a whole has reached, which means that a man must feel that he has at his disposal education, capacity and ability to handle the discoveries of his particular age. He need not have a great deal of money to be able to do that. He need not pile up a quantity of large houses with forty rooms, and a great deal of money and drinks. What a man needs is to eat and drink, and to eat and drink satisfactorily by modern standards is very little. That is not the problem. But he must be able to use, to handle, to have at his disposal the greatest discoveries, the latest discoveries which enhance and develop a man's social personality. And individual personality cannot live a satisfactory life if he is constantly aware of great new discoveries and inventions and possibilities around him from which he is excluded—worse still, that these are threatening him with destruction. The peasant of the Middle Ages did not have very much in comparison to what a modern farmer has; the artisan in his guild did not have for his use what the modern worker has. But he understood and controlled what he was doing. We, the great majority, do not. Marxism demands a universal education of all men in the achievements of modern society. It can be done, easily, but only when the masses of men and women are in control of society. Today, a minority has as its first concern the preservation of its rights and its privileges, i.e., the maintenance of the capital relation.

## The Modern Social Personality

So you see the good life demands a feeling that you are moving, you and your children. You must have a sense of movement and of overcoming difficulties within your organism; and if you are doing that, it does not matter what your wages are as long as you have a certain elementary level of material welfare. You must have a sense of movement, the sense of activity, the sense of being able to use or on the way towards understanding and controlling what makes your life. I do not mean gadgets the way the Americans play with things; I mean things that really matter. This is you personality; this is your social personality; and when this is taking place, although in certain countries they may have two or three times the amount of goods and utilities that you have, yet you can have the good life. You go to a country like Ghana where the general level is even lower than what it is here, but you look at the people, you listen to them, you see what they are doing; you get a sense of movement and activity; they are going somewhere. They will have troubles of course; that does not matter. The Greeks had plenty of troubles.

An American woman told me once that she forgot herself and told an audience of white women in the United States—she was a Negro woman—speaking to them she said, "When I look at you all, I am sorry for you because although whites are oppressing us and giving us trouble, I am actively on the move; every morning I am doing something, but you all are just sitting down there watching." It is not the complete truth, but it is a great part of the truth. This is some idea of what I mean by what is the good life—the individual in relation to society. It is *not*, it never has been, merely a question of what the vulgarians call "raising the standard of living." Men are not pigs to be fattened.

## The Welfare State

Now I want to take the opposite. What, in Washington, in London, in Moscow, what is their conception of the good life for society? Welfare State. Khrushchev, totalitarian as he may be, claims that he is more for welfare than the rest, because in England and in America people can say, "What you are doing is not for welfare. It makes us more miserable." But when Khrushchev tells them in Russia such and such is for their welfare, everybody says yes or says nothing at all; so that they have more of a Welfare State than anywhere. (laughter) Everybody, every government, is agreed today that the state is for the benefit of the community and particularly of the poorer classes of people. That all are agreed upon. I want to take the most important and most highly developed Welfare State of all—Great Britain. I give you an example of that and then we will take Russia.

American journalists are the finest in the world (everything dealing with the masses Americans are extremely good at). They say that in Britain they see after you "from womb to tomb." (laughter) That is an absolute fact, with one reservation. As soon as a mother knows that she has conceived in Great Britain, she can go to the doctors; they will examine her and see after her and she will be able to get what is necessary—proper food and medical attention and so forth free of charge. When children are born, they have the opportunity to go to a good school. Modern systems of education change, but in Britain they have a sense of tradition. They try to be modern, but there is a discipline and a reserve and decency characteristic of these people—(it can be very irritating when you deal with them as grownups); it is very useful in schools; it helps the children to acquire some sort of social personality. (laughter)

If you are unemployed you will be able to go to local relief and be treated not with indignity. At a certain age you have an old age pension. In between, any illness—the most expensive operation—you go to a hospital, they see after you. I know very poor people who have had operations which would cost five hundred to six hundred pounds—absolutely impossible for them without the Welfare State. The doctor writes a prescription, you pay a shilling for each prescription and you get whatever it is.

If you live in the United States and you have to get some antibiotics, you go to the doctor and pay him three dollars; but when you go to the drug store and he gives you the prescription and tells you seventeen dollars, you knees get weak. But in England they just hand it over the counter—one shilling—what it is. Furthermore, if you are on strike, in many districts in England the local municipality (please understand I am making no reference whatever to local problems and local strikes. I have nothing to do with that. If I want to do that I will put up a notice and let everybody know I am going to speak on that and then express myself freely. You have not come here for that. I want to make that clear)— in many municipalities in England, Labour is in power, and many of the houses are municipal houses, quite a number of them. Often when there is a strike the Labour municipality, which has a lot of trade union members, meets and decides that for the duration of the strike they are not going to collect any rent for the municipal houses; whereupon the employers swear that public money is being misused, and the munici- palities say, "We are the majority here. We do what we like." (laughter)

## The Shop Stewards Movement

That is the situation. There is no doubt about it that the extreme misery and poverty which was characteristic of Great Britain during the thirties has, to a substantial degree, been eliminated. Has it brought peace and happiness? Those workers are hostile to their employers to a degree that astonishes those whose philosophy is confined to the higher standard of living. It is in England you have the Shop Stewards Movement, two hundred and fifty thousand of them. There was something about them on the radio this afternoon. I do not know if you heard of the strikes in Great Britain—the recent dockers' strike for example. I am absolutely certain that the official trade union leaders have nothing to do with it at all. The large majority of strikes in Great Britain are organized by shop stewards and local leaders. Having organized and started the strikes, they go to the trade union leaders and say, "You now make it official." The leaders have no choice. Let no one believe that I cannot substantiate this. I can send you to date and place. The struggle in Great Britain now is not so much between the government and the employers and the mass of Labour workers at all. It is between the mass of organized labor and the trade union officials; and part of the defeat of the Labour Party in the last election was certainly due to the growing feeling in the community that the trade union leadership and the Labour Party cannot control the workers and the shop stewards.

You can have little idea of what goes on in British industry, particularly when there is full employment. If a fellow does not like this job here, he simply walks out and goes next door and gets a job. That is absolutely ruinous for capitalism, with the result that serious journals say, "What we really want in this country is at least seven hundred thousand unemployed. Otherwise, we will never be able to have any order and discipline."

At Standard's, an automobile plant in Coventry, two or three years ago, there was the most notorious example. The head of Standard said, "I have eleven thousand men making motor cars. Nine thousand could make the same number of motor cars and make them better if I introduce automation." He said, "I propose to introduce automation and I will have to dismiss two thousand workers. It is for the benefit of the country. We will be able to improve our export trade, etc."

You should have heard what took place. There is a man with whom I was very friendly at the time. He is a Marxist like myself. His brother-in-law is not a Marxist. His brother-in-law passes remarks about Marxists like me, but this man suddenly began to utter statements like this: "I have been working at that plant there for some ten years now. All this big improvement and all this automation that he is going to bring and all the money it is going to cost, we put it there; we, all of us, we put it there; we know that."

He adds, "I am married; I have my wife; I have three children and they are going to school, a good school, and I am buying a house. Now this man tells me that he is going to dismiss two thousand of us. I am probably going to be one and may have to leave Coventry and go to Birmingham. They say there is work in Hull, maybe, or there is work in Yarmouth, or there is work in Brighton." He says, "Not me! I am not going one foot. I am stopping here."

## Two Conceptions of Progress

Now that is the question. This man is not a revolutionary. Yet the Welfare State cannot deal with what is vital to him. It can't. It could deal with him before he is born and just as he is born and while he is a boy. (laughter)

And when he leaves work on an afternoon it can say, "Well, you can get extra education, and the London County Council will have classes; and when you get old we will see after you; and when you die, if nobody can do anything for you, we will bury you." But what happens to him between seven in the morning and half past three to four in the afternoon in the process of production, that the state cannot do anything about. That is where the majority of men live the most intensive part of their lives. That is the problem. A socialist is not a man who is a good man and wishes people well—I hope he is, but that is not what is important. There are many Conservatives who are good men. They obey all the Commandments and wish other people well, but that does not solve the perpetual crisis in production. What is to be done with that man during these eight hours? What are you to say to this man who says, "I refuse absolutely to be pushed around in this way"? And these Standard workers went very far. I haven't the papers by me, but some day or other I am going to publish extracts from them. The *Evening News*, the *Evening Standard*, the *Times* and other papers said in horror: "What is it? You are opposed to progress? We must have progress." And the workers say, "All right! Why dismiss us? Bring it in and we would not have to work so hard." (laughter) One of them says, "Sometimes we have to work hard, well, we have to work hard. But if you bring in the thing, don't dismiss anybody. We would not have to work so hard. Maybe tomorrow we will have to work hard again." The Editor, I think it was the Editor, of the *Evening News* nearly collapsed. He said, "These men will ruin the country. How can you be opposed to progress?" (laughter) They made a big fuss and in the end the workers had to be satisfied with severance pay.

What these workers were saying was this: "If you want to bring in automated machinery here, before you announce it, come and tell us. We work here, you know. Tell us about it. Before you bring in what you are going to bring, tell us. We will discuss it with you and see how and when it should be brought in." Their idea was this: "Well, some people will be dismissed, we know. Maybe this fellow here, maybe he wants to move. This other fellow is a young man, not too particular; let him go. This old man should be sent home altogether." They insisted: "We will fix it up and we will arrange it." Whereupon—and this thing is going on all over the place—the Standard employer says, "You want to tell me what to do with my property!" And they tell him, "That is exactly what we want to do." (laughter) You think those dockers in England—I read about the strike and I know the dockers well—you think they are on strike for ten cents or nine pence more a day? Strikes don't take place for that. They are the result (I am not referring to any strike in Trinidad and Tobago), they are the result of a long process of irritation and antagonism between the two of them that ultimately explodes. This thing has been studied; it is characteristic everywhere.

## Men of the Future

Some two or three years ago at a place called Briggs in London, the government appointed Mr. Justice Somebody to make an investigation. I have the report somewhere. It is in some respects one of the most comic documents that you can read. Those workers, from a certain point of view—from another point of view it is disorderly—those workers have had about three hundred and fifty unofficial strikes in a year. The trade union leaders have nothing to do with that. The strike is started and he in the office has not heard a word at all. (laughter) So the Justice examines. This is what he reports. Those workers carry on lotteries; in six months they have raised about eighty thousand dollars. What have they done with it? They have spent about fifty thousand in giving prizes. The Judge asks them, "What did you do with the rest?" And they told him "Sinews of war." "What are these sinews of war?" "Well, strikes, our own, and to help people if they have strikes, to publish newspapers and so on. We just used it up." Are they Communists? The Judge said, "No, they were not. There were Communists among them but they were not a Communist body."

You see, they have reached a stage in England, the United States and France where, owing to the size and the complicated nature of modern productive industry, it is impossible really to control the workers. You cannot control twenty thousand workers in a plant. You just can't. You can work with them. You get them to work by careful handling; but they will do as much as they want to do and they will do no more; and by and large, except there is a lot of unemployment on the way when the employer has the upper hand, they will do it in much the way that they want to. There are slack periods when they are defeated, but there are periods—and each side knows it well enough—when the employer has a chance to make large profits. And then they squeeze him. This thing goes on interminably. The Welfare State can do nothing about it. As a matter of fact, the more welfare, the more those workers carry on in the factories because they are not living from hand to mouth. Now the employer says that they want him to run the plant in the way that they want, and he says, "You are abusing unionism. I have my property; the government authorizes me to have property. I bought it with my money; my father left it for me. Go to the government. You will see the stamp. This is mine and by law I have a right to run it as I please. Apart from factory regulations, I can do what I like with my own."

He is absolutely right, absolutely right in his contention. He is as right as the slave owner was in 1861. The slave owner said, "This slave is my property. I own him. Look at the papers that I signed for him. Look at the government stamp on it." He said, "Look in the laws, you will see it." Bishops and parsons who read the Scripture said, "Look! St. Paul said, 'Slaves, obey your master.'" (laughter) The slave owner had every justification by law, tradition and custom. There was only one thing that was wrong. The slave said, "I am not going to be a slave anymore." And it was the slave who caused the Civil War. North and South met repeatedly and came to agreements but they could not get the slave to agree not to run away up to the North. That split the whole thing wide open and that is the situation we are in at the present time.

You know, there are people who, when they hear this or read it, will go red in the eyes and hoarse in the voice and scream, "Communist." Treat them with contempt. Here we are in the midst of the most terrible crisis society has ever known. What is wrong? I am giving you an analysis of the facts based upon the philosophy of history and the political method known as Marxism. You have a right to know. You ought to know. And whoever does not want you to know is not only an enemy of Marxism. He is your enemy, wishes to keep you in intellectual ignorance and mental slavery.

## The Russian Planned Economy No Exception

Now I want to go rapidly over to Russia. The same thing I have described is going on in Khrushchev's country. That is what too many people do not know. You have to be able to read their documents. And I have been taught how to read them. First of all, the Russians are masters at double talk. And secondly, you have to know industry and labor relations in order to be able to read these documents. People have sat down and gone through their documents with me. They have said, "If Russia has a modern electronics plant, which they must have in order to make airplanes, and a modern steel plant and modern plants of various kinds to make those planes and satellites, etc., then nothing on earth will prevent the workers in them behaving in much the same way that workers behave in Detroit, in Washington, in Coventry and elsewhere." And they take up the Stalinist documents and they say, "You see this? You see that? That is what that means. You see this? That is what it means."

This is the essence of Marxism. We study the economic relations and try to come to conclusions about them. And in a nutshell our view is that when the decisive forms of industry are massive organizations of thousands of workers, the capital relation, that is to say, properly owned and controlled as in the days when a hundred workers formed a big plant, the capital relation breeds perpetual strife. It is the need to put an end to this strife which is one of the most potent causes of totalitarianism. If the rulers of society can settle this problem, then Marxism will have failed. The totalitarians cannot settle it. Not only Poland and Hungary but Russia itself proves that. The more highly developed the industry, the more you create these masses of workers who are determined to handle the situation in their own way; and one of the things that complicates the situation in Russia—particularly in the old days, despite all the ferocious laws that Stalin used to pass—was that the factory employer had to produce so much or he went to Siberia. (laughter) That was a serious matter for him. So that Stalin would pass regulations that workers who came late three times would be sent to prison for so long, and so forth. But those regulations could not apply for the simple reason that the factory manager who had a certain amount to produce at the end of the year, if he did not produce it he was in trouble. If he had a department with thirty or forty workers who were following more or less the leadership of one or two gifted workers and gifted organizers, then when these came in half an hour late, he did not send them to prison. Why should he do that? He said, "Well, try to come in early next time, boys, but get on with the work." He wanted production and they understood it. Both of them understood one another.

## The Problem to Be Solved

I will give you one example of what you could read in Khrushchev's report in 1957. I am a little bit behind hand in documents, being away from London for so long, but the thing is going on all the time. In this document Khrushchev says, "Trade union leaders and party members have now to mobilize themselves and not keep telling us that everything is fine when in reality production is in disorder." What does this fantastic complaint by Khrushchev. mean? It has been explained to me by experts and I have written a whole chapter of a book on it, written and published too. What has happened is this: the Russian workers have made the factory employers and the Communist Party and the trade union leaders and organizers accept certain conditions, and having forced them to accept the conditions, these fellows, when they were asked from above what was going on, sent back to say, "Everything is fine." But Khrushchev complains that it is not so fine. Why? The plan has said that so much production should come from such a plant in such and such time. The workers say, "Impossible." And if twenty thousand workers say that it is impossible to produce two hundred cars every day, they can only produce one hundred and fifty, nothing in the world can make them produce two hundred. What the workers do is to produce one and fifty for three, four, five months. If you try to force them, then the machinery or the assembly line mysteriously breaks down, and you produce zero. But there is incentive pay; the more you produce over a certain number, what is called the norm, the more money you get. So then the plan says two hundred, but they say, "No, one hundred and fifty." And they insist it is one hundred and fifty because (I know them in Detroit and other places) if the managers give too much trouble, as I say, the assembly line will break down; and if production is urgently needed, then the managers do not make any trouble after that because you cannot find out who is responsible for this when you have about twenty thousand workers. So they insist on bringing it down to one hundred and fifty. After it is established at one hundred and fifty, then any time you go up ten, you get a little extra money for that. So that whereas the plan had two hundred as the norm and extra money for over two hundred, these workers reduced it to one hundred and fifty and then begin to get extra money for one hundred and sixty, one hundred and seventy. They keep going up. When Khrushchev and these others ask the Communist Party and Communist trade union leaders, "How is everything?" they say it is fine. They don't want to get themselves in trouble with twenty thousand workers. As you read the reports you see what I am assured of—and now I have learned to read a bit, though I do not read so well as experienced workers—that once you establish these huge organizational operational factories and structures, the behavior of the workers is dictated by the structure, the production relations dictated by the structure. It is the same everywhere—Welfare State, democratic or totalitarian. Whatever the rulers have to give, they give you outside of the plant. But the worker inside the plant is driven to a hostility which is tearing society apart.

Let me sum up in terms which you should study and work at until they are an instinctive part of your outlook and method of thought:

(a)  All development takes place as a result of *self-movement*, *not* organization or direction by external forces.

(b)  Self-movement springs from and is the overcoming of antagonisms *within* an organism, not the struggle against external foes.

(c)  It is not the world of nature that confronts man as an alien power to be overcome. It is the alien power that he has himself created.

(d)  The end towards which mankind is inexorably developing by the constant overcoming of internal antagonisms is *not* the enjoyment, ownership, or use of goods, but self-realization, creativity based upon the incorporation into the individual personality of the whole previous development of humanity. Freedom is creative universality, *not* utility.

Now I don't want to give the impression in these talks that it is economic relations alone that are decisive. Life is a totality. All we say is that economic relations are the basis. You have to begin there. Why? Because for Marxists economic relations are between people and people; property relations are relations between people and things. And the relations between people and people, between managers and workers in production, are for us Marxists decisive. For example, there are bitter conflicts over the distribution of the product, who will get how much, the division in consumption. Marxism says that if in the process of production there is domination of one set of people, workers, by managers (or owners), then consumption—the distribution of the product—will follow the relations of production—domination of one section of society by another. And we believe that although the connection is not direct, in all aspects of social life, remote though they may be from production, the influence of production relations is felt.

## The Exploitation of Sex

That is one of the reasons why I introduced the exploitation of sex, the exploitation of class and the exploitation of race. I wish to deal very briefly with each of them from a political point of view as to the relation between the traditional society under which we live and the new society which I believe is necessary if society is not to collapse completely. For many centuries women were the most oppressed section of society, and it is common knowledge, common talk, writing among philosophers, that a society was usually to be judged by the position that women occupied in it. And by the way, I would like to say that the nineteenth-century belief that the ancient Greek society treated its women very badly has now been proved to be quite false. These nineteenth century writers had it in their heads and they transferred it to the history they were studying.

Within recent years, however, particularly in the United States, women have won every conceivable legal equality that it is possible to have. Not in England. In England women are working side by side with the men in the factory. They do the same work morning and afternoon, but at the end of the week he gets more pay than she, and he insists upon it. He gives some rigmarole story that women are either wife—which means they get money from their husbands—or they are not married—that means they are living at home; and he, the man, has responsibilities. Whatever the reason, that is the differentiation. In America it does not exist, legally. But when you examine it, this is what happens. There are certain industries—radio, television and such like—which are practically exclusively reserved for women, and whereas a man in one of the big plants will get sixty or seventy dollars a week, the women in these plants get thirty-five dollars a week. So that the segregation is taking place and the discrimination, although not as crudely and as openly as in Great Britain. Now you must understand: in the United States, where the sentiment of equality is extremely powerful, this kind of discrimination breeds a fury in the women who are submitted to it of which you have little conception.

## The Sex War

But there are even greater problems. There is the question of the relation between men and women. This society states that they are equal. Middle class women in particular go to universities and live a life of complete freedom. They have their own latch keys; they drive motor cars about; they go to school; they take exams, they don't take exams; they go to Europe; they do exactly as they please. When they come out of the university they marry and then, almost automatically—you should read the writings of Pearl Buck on this question—almost automatically—from the sheer weight of the tradition of society, from the functions that men perform, from the conceptions that men still have in their minds of the relationship of men to women—they find themselves at twenty-three, twenty-four, twenty-five, in a position of subordination to which they have not been accustomed from the time that they went to school until they left university. The result is a crisis in the relations between men and women in the United States beyond belief. Everybody knows it. It is called "the sex war." I do not know if any of you have met it before or have been reading about it. Europeans and the rest who are more accustomed to taking things as they are, are astonished at this—at the fact that it is in the country where the women have the greatest amount of freedom—where they have all legal freedom—that the relationship between the sexes has reached the stage that it has.

But there is more. A whole lot of women went into the factory during the war. The men had to go to fight and the women went into the factories and they learned to work; they learned freedom; they learned association with other people; they learned independence that comes from doing work with a great number of others, and at the end of the war they did not want to go back home. However, some of them went and even some of those who stayed have been doing their best not to be thrown back again into the narrow, circumscribed life of bringing up the children, removed from the freedoms and associations and opportunities of learning which they had during the years of the war and the years in the factory. They have acquired a tremendous sense of independence. Divorce is easy and free, practically free. There is no problem in many states. You get lodgings quite easily. The subordinations—when I was a young man, a woman with six or eight children had to take it from a man who beat her and spent all his money on drink; that is not the situation in the United States. If a woman is determined not to put up with any ill-treatment of that kind, she can quite often get out of it. The fact is that she can discipline the man's attitude towards her. He does the best that he can. A new problem, from what I gather, has now arisen all over the United States: a man is able to have a certain attitude to a woman if he is the dominant personality and it is accepted as such. But if he grows up as the dominant personality, if in marriage his conception is that of the dominant personality, and then he meets a wife who is quite as familiar in factory business and general activities as himself, he does not know exactly where he stands. And many young men in the United States are in a serious crisis as to exactly what their attitude should be towards the women to whom they are married. Their fathers had no problem; their grandfathers had still less. A woman had to do what she was told; that was very simple. But today, as in so many other things, the old standards have gone but new standards have not been established, with the result that now in the United States, in all spheres of society, there is a crisis such as you have never had before in the relations of male and female. And this takes place precisely because women have economic opportunities and legal freedom and even social freedom to a degree greater than in most other countries.

## The Totality of the Problem

What is going to solve that? It is the belief of the Marxists that the whole society has run down; that it is not an easy problem even to define clearly, these intimate relations, but that, in the last analysis, crises in intimate relations of this kind spring from a dislocation of society, and the attitudes that people have to the society and to the laws, regulations and values by which they live. What is there—in the society—to live by? There is nothing.

In Germany, Hitler, in defense of the interests of the German national state, said: "Women should be the recreation of the tired warrior." (laughter) He said they must have as many children as possible; the state needed soldiers. In Russia, where they carry the perversion of accepted values to an astonishing degree, they say: in Russia we have absolute equality for women, absolute. That, in a society of such a low economic and cultural level, is of course absurd. Look, in the Soviet political leadership, there have been only two or three women. I believe, from the beginning of the Russian Revolution (1917) to the present day, I can only remember three or four women who were ever in the leading committee. But when you look in heavy industry, in the mines, on the railways, in the steel works, you see any number of them working in heavy industry, in spheres which would never have been allowed in the United States or in Great Britain. In Russia they sent them in and boasted of equality. It is a complete perversion of the ideas of equality.

We have to face a fundamental fact that women in their physical and mental qualities are not inferior to men, but different. They also have the immense burden of bearing children; and women in the professions in particular and in academic studies will tell you that they go side by side with the men up to a certain point, but then they wish to bear children (it is an instinct) and their husbands wish to have a family. The men they were keeping pace with up to this stage now go beyond. The socialist view is that child-bearing is no reason why they should be penalized, but that is the very reason why they should be given extra privileges, in order to be able to maintain themselves in the work they are doing. For us, child-bearing is not self-indulgence. Bearing children and bringing them up is a necessary part of society.

## The Totality of the Solution

Capitalist society does not think in those terms at all. You see, when I speak about the reorganization of industry to stop this merciless warfare that goes on every hour of the day in the big plants, it need not necessarily be a strike. It means a human attitude to the dismissal of workers: who is to go, how many, when. It means a human attitude to the status and work of women. You have this profound dissatisfaction of women with their situation in country after country. America has shown that by giving them legal equality and stating that they have full rights to do whatever they wish in the same way as men, does not solve the problem; it makes it worse than before. Millions of women complain that their life consists of maintaining men in industry and bearing children to work in the industry of the future. They claim that through their husbands they are subordinated to the routines and pressures of the factory as if they were employed there. The beginning of a truly satisfactory relationship in personal lives must begin with a total reorganization of labor relations in every department of life. And by now it is obvious that this can only be done by the workers themselves. There are other aspects of the exploitation of sex, but this is the one I wish to refer to. Despite legal freedoms, the domination and subordination of men in the capital relation leads inevitably to the domination and subordination of women, in the place of work, and in the home. It is in the most advanced of all capitalistic countries, the United States, that the conflict is at its most bitter. What is the way out?

We all know about the exploitation of class. I will give you one example—the hostility that educated people have to members of the working class is beyond belief. Not so much in the United States. There they do not understand political democracy. The American believes that if there is a vote and he has the majority, then he has a right to make you do whatever he wants you to. De Tocqueville noticed that, and it is so up to today. Vote finished; I am the majority; I am the boss. Not so in Great Britain. In Great Britain, if there is a room with five hundred and one people and five hundred are for and one against, for that very reason they will say, give him a hearing, hear what he has to say, and they will give him consideration. They have what I call the democratic temper, which is not necessarily parliamentary.

But in the United States, in social relations, they are very far advanced. I am sure if President Eisenhower at any time walked out of the White House and dropped into some tavern, they would be a little bit started at first, but if he said, "Give me one of the old mild," or bitter, or whatever it is; then sat down and said, "Well, boys, how is it?" in five minutes they would be as thick as thieves and would be asking him, "How is Mamie?" and if he said, "Not so well," one would say, "My old lady too"; and they would talk away as Americans like to talk. (laughter) That is how they are. Not in Britain! They understand political democracy in Britain but not equality in social life. Nevertheless, in the United States and elsewhere—and in Russia also—the attitude against workers as uneducated, as being incapable of handling social problems, is firmly implanted in the minds of the masses of people by the very system of education. People react violently against the idea that workers, as a class, can manage anything, when in reality it is they who organize most of the

work of the world. Foremen and managers are there primarily to discipline workers, to maintain the discipline of the capital relation. Remove
the foremen and the managers from most large plants and the work
would go on, in many cases better. That has been proved over and over
again. The work of the skilled technicians can be learned or incorporated
into the general work. Apart from the fact that today it is quite possible
in advanced countries to give to all a general and technical education.
This is the Marxist view of the future of society.

## New Attitudes and Ideas

What we have to overcome are fundamental prejudices which are the
heritage of previous societies and are today maintained for the power
and privileges of a minority. There are people who are bitterly opposed
to the way in which women are made to see after young children—babies
and children up to the time they are ten or eleven. They say that instills
into the mind of the child that, in regard to such matters as comfort and
material needs, he must look to women for them; but for other things—
to go out to play games and work, etc.—he must look to men; so that
by the time he is twelve years old, his mental attitude is corrupted by a
certain attitude to women. And it is much the same in regard to workers.
The plain fact of the matter is that society has to produce ways and means
of stopping these ceaseless conflicts in industry, in factory after factory
in Great Britain, in the United States and France and everywhere else.

Those are the fundamental problems of our society and the first
necessity is to put aside the prejudice against workers as workers. During
the war, Lord Beaverbrook was put in charge of plane production in
England and the people have told me how he carried on. He would come
to the plant, line up everybody and say, "Who are the shop stewards
here?" They would stand out and he would ask, "What is it you want
to improve production?" They would say, "We want this and this and
that." He would tell the employers, "You do what they say," and go his
way. When the pressure came and they wanted production, they knew
where to go for it. But as soon as the war was over, back they went to the
old capitalist way.

Among many members of the middle class, the professional men
in particular, there is a sort of horror of workers and the idea of their

playing a dominant role in society, when in reality they run the railways; they make the steel; they produce the wheat; they grind the flour; they give us electricity; and whenever society collapses they are the ones who have to put it together.

Marxism is not an abstract ideal. It envisages change in its examination of reality. The attitude to workers is changing. One of the most important aspects of contemporary society is the mechanization of clerical work. I heard the other day with great interest that there are in America white collar workers (or black-coated workers), girls with high heels, who are on the picket lines. These girls, who used to do the typing and the writing, find that they are becoming proletarianized. Employers bring in machines—I expect they have some of them here— and the girls are not paid by the week anymore. They come into the big plants and go into the office upstairs and they are paid by the hour. Mechanization, automation, is taking over the work that they used to do, with the result that they are joining unions and are going on picket lines with the workers whom formerly they used to despise: here we have another example of capitalism producing its own grave-diggers.

## The Middle Class

These are fundamental problems of modern society. There are middle class people here who speak of the workers as if they were some kind of *manicou* or lizard. (laughter) These people are hundreds of years behind the times, hundreds of years behind the times. You have to watch the worker's function in society and the dependence of society upon the fundamental functions that he carries out and his capacity to handle his own affairs. That is what is to be examined, and the professional classes in particular have nothing to lose from a socialist society. What have they got to lose? The employers have a lot to lose. People who own property. That is obvious. But what has the professional class got to lose from a socialist society? Do they believe that the workers, having come to political power, will at once begin to hate doctors and dentists and lawyers? Probably the lawyers will not have much to do, but they will find something else to do, that is all. (laughter) This social prejudice is a heritage of many generations and Marxism believes that only a new society will change it. It is unsuitable to the conditions of modern existence.

## The Exploitation of Race

The last one I wish to take up is the exploitation of race. I am not going to speak about the Negro Question and Africa. You are familiar with that. I want to speak of the way in which today the race question is a great political question apart from the question of Africa. I can just outline the main points.

Number one: historically it is pretty well proved now that the ancient Greeks and the Romans knew nothing about race. They had another standard—civilized and barbarian—and you could have a white skin and be barbarian and you could be black and civilized. Those were the standards that they understood. It is said further that the conception of dividing people by race begins with the slave trade. This thing was so shocking, so opposed to all the conceptions of society which religion and philosophers and others had (despite St. Paul and his, "Slaves, obey your masters"), that the only justification by which humanity could face it was to divide people into races and decide that the Africans were an inferior race. That is the beginning of the modern conception of people being divided into different races. It did not exist before. It is going to take a lot of trouble before it is finished with. Anyway, Nkrumah and others in Africa are doing a pretty good job to clear up that mess over there, and that will help.

That is not all. Hitler introduced the conception of the master race. You see, the world does not make progress and stay there. Either it goes on or it goes back, and Hitler introduced into Europe the most reactionary concept of the master race, which had originated in colonialism. He used it as an ideological instrument for murdering millions of people.

There is another concept originating from colonialism—the alleged superiority of one system which entitles it to rule allegedly inferior systems. The imperialists used that doctrine. Today the Russians dominate half of Europe, which does not belong to them. They are the masters; there is no talk there about "in future when you learn to govern" as the British will say, "we will go and leave you." Not with the Russians. They are there; they are going to stay there. As far as may be seen they intend to be masters of that half of Europe, and from the fuss they are making about Berlin, they mean to terrorize the other half. Their ultimate aim is to drive the Americans out of Europe with the result that, not under the name of race, but in the name of a superior society, the Russian state is steadily establishing itself as a master race in Europe. Their army and their secret police and their agents rule in the satellite countries. There are some short-sighted people who turn a blind eye to all this and claim that the Russian system is progress. To me the argument comes strangely from the mouths of those just emerging from centuries of colonialism. The Europeans have paid a terrible price for allowing these ideas to establish themselves unchecked in European thought. Let us see to it that we do not make the same mistake.

Look at race and the question of Chinese and Japanese. Before the war, on the West Coast of America, California in particular, they spoke incessantly of the "yellow peril," so that as soon as the war broke out, government moved in on the Japanese, put them in concentration camps and stripped them of their property. Now the war is over, Mao Tse-Tung and the Communists become masters of China, establish Chinese national independence, except for Chiang Kai-Shek fooling around in Formosa. Thereupon the American attitude changes. Look at television, listen to the radio, look at movies, you see a lot of pictures of Chinese and Japanese girls marrying American men, American girls marrying Japanese men. Why this change? Why no more "yellow peril"? Because the problem now is: which way is Japan going to go, with the democratic West, or is it going to go Communist and join up with China? That is the problem now: political, not racial. They are doing their best to win over the Japanese. The question of race has subsided. That is why they took Hawaii and made it an American state. The Japanese—they and all the Orient—kept on saying, "You all are taking everybody, you have all sorts of states, but why don't you take the Hawaiians? They want to come in. Why don't you take them? It is because they are not all of them white that you don't." And under that pressure, and with sympathetic elements inside America, they made Hawaii the fiftieth state. You see, they exploited race as long as it was useful. Now it is dangerous and they drop it. But if tomorrow Japan goes Communist or becomes a close ally of Communist China, as sure as day the yellow peril business is going to be raised again. So that is the way, you see. Our masters exploit these fundamental relations in society: sex, class and race. They are always there to be used by reactionary elements, and Russia exploits these in her own way.

I have gone into them not as profoundly as I might if I took up each alone. But I was concerned to show you that Marxism is not merely concerned with economic questions and economic production—production relations—as so many people think. It is clear that all these problems are posed in the West Indies, if not sharply today then certainly tomorrow. You will judge. I have given America as the chief example, but in Britain and elsewhere they are there.

## Eternal Vigilance

Progress is not automatic. Hitler threw Europe back. To fight him it was necessary to fight the theory of race. But that theory can rise again. These reactionary concepts can become more acute than they have ever been in the past, not because they are ineradicable from human nature, but because of the fundamental disorder in modern society. You see what the Marxist solution is. Marxists envisage a total change in the basic structure of human relations. With that change these problems will not be solved overnight, but we will be able to tackle them with confidence. Such are the difficulties, contradictions and antagonisms, and in the solution of them society moves forward and men and women feel they have a role in the development of their social surroundings. The individual can find a more or less satisfactory relation to the national and to the world community. It is in this movement that we have the possibility of a good life.

But if, on the other hand, reaction grows and the question of the freedom of women and the question of the equality of classes and the question of differences of race begin to be used—as they are bound to be used by reactionary elements in the defense of positions which are no longer defensible—society becomes sick unto death. The individual cannot find an easy relation either to the state or to his fellow men. Not only are we affected in war, in economics, and in politics. The turmoil the world is in reacts upon our most intimate consciousness in ways we are not aware of. And every succeeding day brings us nearer and ties us closer to the decisive forces and conflicts of the modern world. What has suddenly erupted in Cuba is going to place many of the things I am talking about before you, first for your discussion, and sooner or later for your decision. We were not able to choose the mess we have to live in—this collapse of a whole society—but we can choose our way out. I am confident that these lectures will help and not hinder.

Next time we will conclude. (applause)

# Chapter Six
## Thursday, 25th August, 1960

MR. CHAIRMAN, LADIES AND GENTLEMEN:

This is the last of the series of lectures. I would like to say, first of all, that I have given many series of lectures at classes of one kind or another, not only when I was a regular teacher, but in the course of an active political and literary life. Looking back over them I believe that, taken as a whole, although I have given classes and lectures at universities, this is about the most important and the most satisfactory to me—and I hope to you—that I have given in the course of the last twenty-five years. (applause)

I have not said everything: if I had said a lot of the things I have omitted to say, I would not have been able to say many of the things that I have said. I shall try to make clear in the course of this evening's final lecture what I have been endeavoring to do. But all things considered, I would like to say that I am profoundly grateful to the Trinidad Public Library and their Adult Education Program for giving me the opportunity to speak as freely as I have been able to do. I cannot imagine any other forum anywhere in which I would have been able to speak with more freedom than I have been able to speak here on a very controversial subject, and that is a matter of great importance. I hope that when the shriekers and the barkers start to yell, as will inevitably happen, all of you will rise to the defense of freedom of speech in the Adult Education Program. (applause)

I have been very careful how I have spoken. I am trying to put forward certain ideas which are not only of theoretical and intellectual importance, but are of objective importance in the world of today and still more of tomorrow. They are going to be published. My wife and I are working very hard on the scripts, and when the time comes we shall be satisfied that in the course of three years here we have been profoundly grateful for the opportunity, and feel that in this particular series of lectures as published we shall have left something behind us which will last. (applause)

Tonight I am going to stick pretty closely to the program, and when question time comes I hope the reporters and those who are recording will take everything. I have not only to go through the program but also to fill certain gaps and connect various strands, which may have been loose.

## How We See Ourselves

Now the first thing is "How We See Ourselves," and I have given a list of modern writers—a famous and remarkable list, as you can see. I am going to spend a minute or two on each—no more—in order to underline—that is all I can do—how the most gifted and most sensitive minds of our period see the world in which we live. There is Rimbaud, a French poet, one of the greatest poets of the modern age. He fought in the Paris Commune as a boy of sixteen and then he went wandering over Europe. He had a homosexual relationship with Verlaine, another famous French poet. They wandered about in Belgium and Holland; one got jealous and cut up the other with a knife. One went to hospital, the other one went to jail. He finally left Europe—I do not think he wrote any more poetry after he was about twenty-five. He found his way to Abyssinia, where he traded, and lived with a native woman. He died at the age of thirty-seven. His most remarkable poem is *A Season in Hell*, in which he describes the homosexual relationship with Verlaine.

This is one of the greatest poets of the last hundred years. You can read him in translation and it is almost as fine. Writers are often erratic people in their social behavior but few have been quite so erratic as Rimbaud. Rimbaud's idea of writing poetry was the most remarkable I know. By means of drugs or by some process, he aimed to derange his mind, to turn his mental faculties upside down, to become crazy; and then he wrote what all the world recognized as magnificent poetry. In other words, you see, what is taking place here is *a total rejection of the standards and values of the age.* He has to get himself into a frame of mind in which he sees everything the opposite way, so to speak, and what is still more remarkable, when he gets in this frame of mind and writes, it is recognized by the public that he has made deep penetration into the realities of modern society.

## Joyce

The next one is James Joyce. His first novel is *Portrait of the Artist as a Young Man*, in which he shows how he got away from the Catholic Church. His second is *Ulysses*, one of the greatest books of our day. It describes the lives of a few Irish people in twenty-four hours—one day—and Joyce penetrates deep into the realities of the human mind and human life, into the depths that lie under the surface behavior—to such a degree that the book was banned for many years. It had to be privately printed, and only recently a judge in the United States and another one in Britain decreed that the book can be published for ordinary reading. Again we have a total rejection of contemporary standards and values. Joyce went still further. He wrote another novel called *Finnegans Wake*, which I can't read. It is written in a language entirely his own. So that he not only rejects standards and values but ultimately the language that the ordinary people speak and in which he had written for years.

## Lawrence

The next is D.H. Lawrence. Lawrence found that men were so lacking in masculinity—particularly bourgeois educated men—that it was necessary for the world once more to try to recover the real profundity of the sexual relation before life could become healthy again. Meanwhile, his ladies, the women, they fall in love with gamekeepers. I remember a story called *Son*, in which an American woman falls in love with an Italian peasant who was cleaning up the yard. He has another story significantly called *The Virgin and the Gypsy*. Here is one of the finest of modern prose writers, and this is his view of society. You cannot reject Lawrence. It is true that being a Protestant Englishman he rather shrieks and yells about things which people on the Continent would take a little more lightly, but what he has to say about the sexual degeneration of modern society is as valid today as it was when he wrote it.

## Proust

The next is Marcel Proust, who wrote the famous novel, *In Search of Lost Time*. It is one of the finest pieces of literature produced during the last fifty years, and it is one of the great novels of the world. It consists of the merciless picture of the degeneration of the French aristocracy after the French Revolution of 1848. One of the most striking characters is a homosexual.

## Eliot and Pound

Next Mr. T.S. Eliot. What is the name of his famous poem? What does he think the world is? He calls it *The Waste Land* and the world ends "not with a bang but with a whimper." It does not even make a gesture. It just crawls off into some hole.

Ezra Pound is one of the great literary figures of the day. He and T.S. Eliot have had a greater influence on the shaping of the English language into the modern style than any other two authors, these two Americans. Pound's poetry is very difficult, but I will give you some idea of his life. He went to Europe somewhere in the early years of the century. He worked with Eliot at destroying the Miltonic and Wordsworthian and Tennysonian traditions in English literature. They put an end to that. Pound was anti-Semitic; he hated Jews. He hated capitalism. He preached some fantastic economic theory of social credit. He knew nothing about economics, but he continued to write essays and some poetry about it. In his poetry he translated from the Latin, from the medieval French, from the Chinese, linking them all together, always hostile to the existing standards of modern society. He went to Italy. When the war broke out, he joined the Italian Fascists, and he broadcast on the Fascist side against America, his native country. When the war was over, he was taken to the United States, a prisoner. Obviously he was a traitor. What to do with this man? They put him in jail, and while in jail he published a volume of poetry, and judges of American poetry said this was the best for that year. (laughter) I don't know if he is still in jail or if they have let him out on parole. I don't know what has happened to him. For my part, he may as well be out. I doubt if he will convince anyone of his political ideas.

That is a picture of one of the most gifted literary men of the twentieth century. No history of the literature of the century could be written without paying tribute to Ezra Pound.

## Sartre

The next is Jean-Paul Sartre, the Existentialist. He believes that the prevailing condition of the human mind is anguish. He has written a famous philosophical work, *On Being and Nothingness*. The name of two of his books are *Nausea* and *Flies*, and I assure you they are well named. Sartre is the most gifted, learned and versatile of post-war writers. He flirts with Communism and is an inveterate enemy of bourgeois society.

## Hemingway and Faulkner

There is the famous Hemingway. Just look at the names of Hemingway's books: *A Farewell to Arms;* he is finished with all that war. Another of his books: *Men Without Women.* The next one, *Green Hills of Africa.* He goes there shooting wild animals, and when he is finished he goes to Spain to write *Death in the Afternoon*, a panegyric on bull fighting. The Civil War breaks out in Spain, and he goes there and writes another book: *For Whom the Bell Tolls.* That is his mentality. (laughter) When the Second World War broke out, he went again and wrote *Across the River and into the Trees.* Hemingway has no use for enthusiasm, liberal values, everything that we may call "uplift." He has no use for that at all; that is the basis of his famous style. Hemingway is interested in things that you can touch and you can see, and in elemental emotions that will deceive nobody. He is a Nobel Prize winner.

Faulkner is another American writer. His themes are rape, perversion of all kinds, incest, murder, suicide, race prejudice, decline of a family, decline of a whole town, decline of a whole province. That is Faulkner—another Nobel Prize winner. Faulkner is a born writer.

## Camus

Another Nobel Prize winner is Camus, a Frenchman who died the other day; he was killed in an accident. Of the two books which made his reputation, one is called *The Stranger*, and the other is called *The Plague*. And one of his famous philosophical books is *L'Homme Révolté* (published in English as *The Rebel: An Essay on Man in Revolt*).

I could spend the rest of the evening describing these modern writers—the finest writers of the day—who paint such a picture of gloom, degeneration, decay, perversion as I don't remember in any previous period of literature.

Some of the American businessmen complained very bitterly some years ago: "These artists never write about us," they said. So one or two people tried to write some novels about them. They didn't succeed.

This is the picture of our age by its most gifted, its most penetrating, its most creative writers. I know their work, most of them (I don't know Pound's work very well; I know the work of the others), and they are some of the finest writers of the last hundred years. Their condemnation of modern society is absolute.

## The Undying Vision

However, those are not the only artists of the time. There are some others, and I have called them examples of "The Undying Vision"; and the people I have chosen are Charles Chaplin; the American movie director, D.W. Griffith; the Russian movie director, Eisenstein; and the famous Spanish painter, Picasso.

Now the one I like to begin with first is D.W. Griffith, not only the greatest movie director in the whole history of movies, but in my opinion the greatest artist of the twentieth century. (I do not count Tolstoy because Tolstoy was dead by 1910.) I believe that in a hundred years' time, when the history of art of the twentieth century is being written, it is these men that will be written about, and not these others. Life is too limited in the vision that the prophets of gloom and doom have of it.

## Birth of a Nation

Griffith was doing his finest work before 1914—his best work was done before 1920 and he went on until about 1930. His audience consisted chiefly of immigrants from abroad who did not know the American language very well. He was using movies as a means of interesting and educating people who were not quite at home in the American civilization. I believe that being a great artist and being compelled to meet the necessities of the great masses of semi-educated people, is the secret of the great discoveries that he made and of the place that he holds today in the history of the cinema. Two of his films I recommend to you, and I sincerely hope that somehow or other they will be brought here. One is called *Birth of a Nation* and it is the history of the Civil War in the United States. In the second part of that picture, Griffith is very harsh on the Negro people. He did not know any better. Most of America thought the same at the time. In the United States today, when the picture is being shown, most of the Negro organizations and many of the White progressive organizations go and picket because they say the picture is anti-Negro. I go early in the morning to see the picture and then come in the afternoon to picket. (laughter)

## Intolerance

Griffith is a very great artist and should not be judged too hastily. Lenin saw this picture, and he wrote a letter to Griffith in his personal handwriting, asking him to come to Russia and take charge of the Russian movie industry. He did not mind that Griffith had shown prejudice against the Negro. Lenin knew that this could be overcome. And in his next picture, *Intolerance*, he made amends. (I hope, Mr. Comma, that you will try to bring to Trinidad *Birth of a Nation* and *Intolerance*. It would be a magnificent contribution to education, both artistic and social, in this country.) (applause) *Intolerance* is a film that lasts about three hours. In it Griffith tells four stories: the story of Christ; the story of the St. Bartholomew Massacre in France in 1572; a story of modern life—workers and employers; and the story of the fall of ancient Babylon. These four stories are not told one after the other. He cuts from one to the other. He has a marvelous eye, and when you see some people riding down a street in Paris in the sixteenth century, you see Paris in the sixteenth century, and you see the people also.

In this film he introduces a rape by a white person of a white girl; so he meant to say, you see, everybody rapes—no, not everyone rapes—but anybody, not only Negroes, can rape. (laughter) At the end of the picture, in the last fifteen minutes, there is Christ going up the hill of Calvary, Christ and the two thieves. And he cuts back from that to the

Massacre of St. Bartholomew, another historic event. And then he cuts again into the history of the fall of Babylon. The girl in the modern story, her boyfriend is falsely accused and is about to be hung and somebody is racing to get him off with a pardon. So that there is a story of Christ and the Crucifixion, there is the Massacre of St. Bartholomew, there is the twentieth century—someone in a motor car racing a train in order to get to the Governor to save this young man's life—and there is the fall of Babylon. After cutting two minutes, two minutes, two minutes, he starts cutting one minute, one minute, one minute, and as somebody has said, you see history pouring over the screen.

I have seen that picture about ten times. My wife has taken notes of each separate scene and the time Griffith gives to it. I am going to write about it some day, but to write about it is not good enough. You have to see it. You have to see them: *Birth of a Nation* and *Intolerance.* And do not let Griffith's anti-Negro attitude in *Birth of a Nation* put you off from one of the great movies of the world.

## Charlie Chaplin

The other man is Mr. Charles Chaplin, one of the great artists of the day and one of the greatest ever known. His early pictures: *Shoulder Arms*, an anti-war picture; *The Immigrant* shows you how the immigrants to the United States were treated; *City Lights*, *The Circus.* All the early ones and a good many of the middle ones—there is nothing like Chaplin on the modern stage or in modern movies at all. And what is Chaplin's fundamental position? It is the same as that of *Don Quixote. Don Quixote* is one of the great novels of the world, among other reasons because Don Quixote, in the days when the modern world was beginning, dressed himself up in armor and went around trying to behave as if he was one of the great knights of old.

Chaplin has done the same thing, only the people he is mocking are not the knights of old. He has dressed himself up in his bowler hat, a morning coat, some big boots, a cane and a fancy waistcoat, and he is mocking bourgeois society and its typical representatives. Those are the people he is laughing at. Don Quixote had made himself an idiot in trying to be a knight of old. But Chaplin says that he is going to be a gentleman. He is very poor and very miserable, but at least he can behave according to the standards and values and high principles of the romanticism of the nineteenth century. Chaplin is going to be a perfect gentleman, and as he bows to the ladies in the most elegant style, he slips on the banana skin and falls down.

That is what he is doing at the time, showing how impossible it is to live according to the standards and values that people talk about. Hemingway will have nothing to do with that at all, absolutely nothing. He wouldn't even attack it directly; he just ignores it. Chaplin is different. He says, "Well, let us live according to these gentlemanly principles if we can." In addition to that, he is a very human person, and when the gentlemanliness, etc., does not work out and Chaplin has to fight or to run for his life, he fights and runs like you or me. But in addition to being so ridiculous, the fundamental human virtues (not the superficial ones) are with Chaplin. And you know his famous endings: after all the trouble, you see him walking off into the distance along the road, into the horizon. He has been in a lot of trouble, he has been defeated, but he is still unconquered, and he is going off. And the next time he turns up as bright as ever. His vision of the good life is undying. His sense of form is unsurpassed, his humanity wide and deep, and I believe that it is his consciousness of the popular audience that gives him his strength.

## Eisenstein

The next one is Eisenstein. His famous film, *Potemkin*, is a film of the 1905 Revolution in Russia, with the famous scene on the steps of Odessa. All the people have come to pay homage to a revolutionary who was killed. The people are on the steps there and suddenly the Czar's soldiers appear at the top and they start to come down. The people rush down the steps, and at a certain time you only see boots—those long top boots, and bayonets, not men anymore; boots and bayonets—the people running and boots and bayonets. This is one of the most famous of modern scenes, and it epitomizes what Czarism stood for in the minds of the Russian people and the people of Europe.

He has made many other films, but none has equaled that. That was done in Russia during the heroic days of the Russian Revolution. You see, what I am saying is that the greatest artists of our day have been people who somehow have found themselves in circumstances in which they did not write or work for the educated intellectual public, as all these other writers do, but found themselves compelled to appeal to the ordinary citizen. What I am telling you is no idiosyncrasy of mine. These men who worked as popular entertainers are today recognized, although some would not go as far as I go.

## Picasso

The last man that I want to speak about is Picasso. I am very sorry that we only have this reproduction here of his painting, *Guernica*, but as a memento of this series I am going to send you, Mr. Comma, a reproduction of *Guernica* large enough to give some idea of the picture. Furthermore, it is made in a material which does not reflect the light and it is washable. I hope you will put it up somewhere in this hall or on the steps coming up, so that people coming to future lectures will see it and remember me. That will be very nice. (applause)

Picasso, I have been told by people who are art critics, as an artist, at least as a draftsman, is of the quality of Leonardo da Vinci and Michelangelo. Nobody could handle a pencil and draw anything better than Picasso. He was a complete master, but for many years Picasso was noted as one of the most gifted of modern artists who, however, experimented. He had a blue period. I think he had a red period. He had a Greek period. He had a Negro period (although he denies it), which does not mean that he painted Negro people, but he imitated or got ideas from Negro sculpture. And this went on, this extraordinary virtuosity and this series of great paintings, until 1937, when Picasso was about fifty.

He is a Spaniard and in 1937 Franco's Air Force wiped out a small city called Guernica. They wiped it out completely. It was an anticipation of atomic and hydrogen bombs. Picasso decided to do a painting of Guernica. For the first time in his career he was moved by social action and he used all this magnificent capacity and technique that he had accumulated to do something which the ordinary person would be able to respond to. Everybody knew of what Franco had done to Guernica. The result is without a shadow of a doubt, if not the greatest, then the most famous painting of the twentieth century. If the Chairman will hold this (picture) with me—afterwards if you wish you can come up and look at it—I will give you some idea of what the painting is like.

In the center of it is a horse, which represents feudalism, reaction, political conservatism of the meanest kind. The horse is in desperate agony, and you know these feudal horses always wore a sort of big cloth over them. Picasso has put a cloth over this horse, but on the cloth he has a lot of what looks like newspaper print, a lot of propaganda they are always filling people up with. Below the horse is a man who has been fighting, who has been defeated. I do not understand that fellow very well; to me, when you look at him, he seems pretty hollow. On the right is a building on fire from the bombs, one woman screaming and another woman running away. On the left is a woman with her child appealing for help to a bull. The bull, I believe, represents the general public, not yet certain of what it can do in regard to this crime but full of power and with rising anger. Other work by Picasso and a drawing by Goya, another great Spanish painter, seem to indicate this. Over the whole is an electric light: the electric bulb of extreme power shows that it is the modern world. But to me, most remarkable of all, there is a Greek face and, attached to the face, an arm holding a lamp, so that in the midst of this chaos and these catastrophes is the lamp of culture and wisdom that was lit by ancient Greece. Picasso places this in probably the most dominant position in the painting. In all the chaos and catastrophe of the modern world, Picasso affirms the undying vision of Greek civilization and the power inherent in the mass of mankind.

## The Artist and the Audience

There is a famous painting by Velasquez called *Las Meninas*, The Maids of Honor. You will see it in a lot of books, reproductions of it. It is a picture of the king and one of the young princesses and the maids of honor, the painter himself and his pictures; a study in composition and light. When we were in London the other day, we went to an exhibition of Picasso. You know that fellow sat down and painted forty-seven different versions of *Las Meninas*. He twisted it all ways and then he turned it round and he looks at it from this point of view and that, he does it in modern style—forty-seven times. I mention that to show you the type that he is. But his greatest painting is *Guernica*. We knew nothing about atomic bombs then; we knew nothing about hydrogen bombs and guided missiles then. But somehow he felt that the destruction of Guernica meant something significant above the ordinary. He got caught up in revolt against what had taken place and the result is this stupendous painting. Picasso's *Guernica* and Chaplin and Griffith and Eisenstein—in the twentieth century they have been able to do what they did because they turned their faces away from the normal educated public who are accustomed to reading the poetry of Eliot and Rimbaud and the novels of Sartre and Proust. They spoke to ordinary men, and the result is the greatest art of our century. To me this signifies a great deal. Picasso calls himself a Communist, but when he draws pictures of the Communists, they raise Cain, because they even tell Communist artists how to paint. But Picasso lives in France. They can't control him, and he paints as he pleases.

Last time I spoke of sex and race and class because Marxism, although it bases itself on economic relations, is a total view of society. And now we have had a glimpse (merely a glimpse) of modern art, to see conflicting currents and where, in my opinion, what I call "The Undying Vision"—that men will do something with themselves—on which side and in what circumstances—that can be found.

## Automation

Now I am going to review finally all that we have been doing, and I hope that you will bear with me if I read some extracts, a thing I do not like to do. But I think we can take it at this stage.

"Science and Industry; the Grandeur of Automation and the Folly of Satellites."

Now some of you, I am sure, know what automation is. Year after year the factories in the United States are being automated. Some of them go to the extreme of having a dozen workers where formerly a thousand worked. That is the latest technical revolution, and it faces mankind, especially workers, with an insoluble crisis under the present social order.

What are you going to do with them? It looks as if in ten or twenty years we will be able to produce with only one-tenth of the present number of workers. I don't know about these bombs and missiles. I am speaking about ordinary human beings and what we need in ordinary life. In ten or twenty years one-tenth of the present population, of the working population of the United States, to take one country, will be able to produce what ten times their number produce today. What is to be done? The average capitalist says, "That is the business of I don't know whom. I am going to have some automation and produce cheaply in order to be able to sell more goods." But the government and the trade unions and those who are concerned with the labor movement are profoundly concerned because there have been enough disorders and conflicts in the labor movement and in production up to this day. To add this new problem means a final catastrophe. And yet I say "The Grandeur of Automation."

## The Universal Man

Now we have discussed in the past the labor question. I have given you some examples. Tonight I want to clinch the question by giving you only two statements. The first is from Marx's *Capital* and I am sure you will admire me for my forbearance, that in six lectures on Marxism I have never quoted him once. The average lecturer on Marxism quotes him six times in each lecture, but I prefer not to do, that. I have aimed at giving you a conception. You will read and find out for yourselves. But I want to read a passage from *Capital*, Volume I, and I am going to read it very carefully. Marx says: "Modern Industry, on the other hand, through its catastrophes imposes the necessity of recognizing as a fundamental law of production variation of work, consequently the greatest possible development in his varied aptitudes."

The labor must be varied; consequently fitness of the laborer for varied work. He should have a technical education; consequently the greatest possible development of varied aptitudes. Then Marx is very specific. He says: "It becomes a question of life and death for society, to adapt the mode of production to the normal functioning of this law. Modern Industry, indeed, compels society, under penalty of death; to replace the detail-worker of today, crippled by lifelong repetition of one and the same trivial operation."

He says society will collapse if it does not replace the detailed worker of today. You have seen Chaplin's film in which he went to work on the assembly line, and what happens to him? Have any of you seen it? What is the name of that film? (Audience: *Modern Times.*) *Modern Times.* It had slipped me. You have seen it here? (Audience: Yes.) Chaplin is doing a certain action all the time, and after a while he can't stop. He just goes on doing it all the time, and then he starts to walk around and he sews buttons on ladies' clothes and he starts to carry out the action again. It is a marvelous satire but satire on a very serious question.

Marx says (continuing): "Crippled by life-long repetition of one and the same trivial operation, and thus reduced to the mere fragment of a man, by the fully developed individual, fit for a variety of labors, ready to face any change of production, and to whom the different social functions he performs, are but so many modes of giving free scope to his own natural and acquired powers."

He says that is what modern industry has to be, or the whole thing will collapse. Now automation demands very highly skilled workers and very highly skilled, though not very many, attendants. Furthermore, it is certain that changes in production will be extremely rapid and Marx says you have to have a worker who is able to adapt himself to these changes—who is so educated that he is fitted for a variety of work, so that as industry shifts and changes and various scientific and other combinations take place, this man is able to adjust himself to any changes, because he is educated to correspond. That is Marxism. That is the theory. *Capital* was written in 1867. Marx foresaw. He says that is where capital is going, and ultimately it will not be able to proceed at all unless you get a working force of this kind. But a working force of this kind is not going to be ordered about by an employer. It is going to take control of industry and that is the socialist society.

The study of Marx's *Capital* is one of the most rewarding studies, and it can and should last a lifetime. Today, 1960, students of automation and of Marxism will tell you that this type of highly-skilled, educated, creative worker is the type that automation must have. He is there already. In the most famous chapter of *Capital*, the chapter before the last in Volume I, one of the greatest triumphs of the human mind (you should know it by heart), Marx shows that the socialist society already exists, under the capitalist covering. Its task now is to break through.

## The Workers Councils

Now the second extract I am going to read is very modern. This is a most respectable book. It is a book on the Hungarian Revolution. It is written by Mr. Melvin Lasky, and it is published for the Congress for Cultural

Freedom. Bertrand Russell, Silone and a lot of very distinguished liberal-minded gentlemen—they have a Congress for Cultural Freedom. (I once wrote an article for one of their papers and I told the Editor, "You will never publish that article in your paper." It was a French magazine. He said, "I will publish. You get it translated." I got it translated. He paid me the money to get it translated. He paid me twenty pounds for the article, and to this day it has not been published. I said, "They will never let you publish that." He said, "I am the Editor." I said, "We will see.")

Anyway, these gentlemen produced this book on the Hungarian Revolution—full of important facts, etc. I am afraid they didn't understand it very well. It takes a lot of trouble to be able to understand things like the Hungarian Revolution. They put some of the facts down, and I want to read for you in relation to this what the Presidium of the National Trade Union Council of Hungary issued as a directive to factories during the Hungarian Revolution. You will remember, please, that, as I have said, this book is "kosher," as the Jews say. This is what the leading body of the Hungarian trade unions has to say:

*The Trade Union Council Presidium recommends that workers and employees* [that means clerical workers] *embark on the introduction of worker-management in factories, workshops, mines and everywhere else. They should elect Workers Councils.*

*(1) Regarding the functioning of the Workers Councils, we recommend that members should be elected by all workers of the factories, workshop, or mine in question. A meeting called to carry out the election should decide the method of election. Recommendations for Workers Council membership should be presented, as a general rule, by the works council or by a worker who commands respect. Depending on the size of the enterprise, the Workers Councils should generally consist of 21–27 members, including proportionate representation of every group of workers. In factories employing less than 100 workers, all workers may be included in the Workers Council.*

*(2) The tasks of the Workers Council. Workers Councils shall decide all questions connected with production, administration and management of the plant . . .*

That, you see, is total. It continues:

*. . . Therefore: (a) it should elect from among its own members a council of 5–15 members, which in accordance with direct instructions of*

*the Workers Council, shall decide questions connected with the manage-
ment of the factory—it will hire and fire workers, economic and technical
leaders;* [That means bookkeepers and engineers. These will take charge
of that.] *(b) it will draw up the factory's production plan and define tasks
connected with technical development; (c) the Workers Council will choose
the wage system best suited to conditions peculiar to the factory, decide
on the introduction of that system, as well as on the development of social
and cultural amenities in the factory; (d) the Workers Council will decide
on investments and the utilization of profits; (e) the Workers Council will
determine the working conditions of the mine, factory, etc.; (f) the Workers
Council will be responsible to all the workers and to the State for correct
management.*

## Socialism or Barbarism

These Workers Councils were formed all over Hungary. And when that
takes place, that is the end of the capitalist mode of production. These
fellows were prepared to take over completely—investments, profits,
wages, working conditions, hire of bookkeepers, hiring of engineers.
Nobody told them about this, you know. Marx said that capitalism would
inevitably come to the stage where the workers would take over. If they
don't or can't, he added, society would relapse into barbarism. Look at
the world we live in and judge.

That is what Marxism is, not an ideal, a utopia in the head, but a scientific doctrine that enables you to examine phenomena, predict developments and so prepare for them, correct yourself when you are wrong,
recognize the limitations of man's possibilities at any particular time or
any particular stage, but recognize also his mastery of all possibilities
within those limitations. For us, that the workers of Hungary were ready
to take over the economy and had won the confidence of farmers and
intellectuals, that is the vindication of our theory and a guarantee of a
high destiny for the great mass of mankind. For non-Marxists, what does
the Hungarian Revolution signify? God only knows.

There are many conclusions to be drawn. I will draw just one or
two. If you have followed with how stage by stage capitalism produces
an organized proletariat, you will recognize the enormous significance
of what took place in Hungary (and by the way, it was taking place in

Poland also). Now it is clear that when the Russian troops smashed up the Hungarian Revolution, they were smashing up the socialist society. You cannot have it both ways. Russian state capitalism couldn't allow Hungarian socialism to exist because Poland was just next door and if this thing had spread, it was going to spread to Russia too. They said, "Finish up with this here. We don't want any of this kind of business." And they sent tanks to smash it to bits.

Now you will remember that everybody was saying that the world was destined for totalitarianism. George Orwell had written a book in which he said *1984* was the date; you know the book—Big Brother and so on. People said that the Russians would get the children and teach them and nobody would be able to teach them anything about freedom and socialism. Then this revolution exploded and showed what the Hungarian people wanted. We respect books, like Rousseau's *Social Contract* and Marx's *Capital*. But books are tested in life. Study books but study also great historical events like the Hungarian Revolution.

## The Government of Workers Councils

Now this book by Lasky does not have the most important resolution that was passed in the revolution, and that was this: when the Hungarian intellectuals saw what was taking place and they saw that the Russians might come back (the original Communist Government was gone), they stopped all their talk about free elections and parliamentary liberties and all that and they said: "Let us have a Government of Workers Councils," and they proposed to make Zoltan Kodaly, the famous Hungarian composer, to make him President. They said, "Everybody knows him, and if he goes and sits and says, 'Well, I am with the Workers Council,' he will stand for Hungary."

The importance of that is this: the intellectuals, the educated, the professional men had to turn to the workers for a government. The army had joined the revolution; the police had fallen apart; the secret police were hiding. The Communist Party and the Communist Government could not be found anywhere, and there were Workers Councils everywhere. So what to do? They said, "Form a Government of Workers Councils." You see, that is the way these things happen. They are the result of the objective actions of millions of people in regard to a definite situation. Simply, there was a situation to be dealt with. That I believe is the highest point yet reached by the Marxist movement.

Some of you say, yes, the society is breaking down; you don't know how many satellites are going round and round and round; we are faced with disaster; there is general decay. You agree to all that. But you sit on the edge and you want it fixed nice and tight so that you can just leave this old society and step into this new one. It does not happen that way. Oh no. It does not happen that way. After all, the first workers state as we know it—very rough and crude—faced great difficulty in 1917. This is only 1960, forty-three years. Look where the Hungarian workers have reached.

Take parliamentary democracy. The Levellers put it forward in 1646. It was 1927 before the British gave the vote to women, and in France the women got it after they had fought in the Resistance Movement I don't think they have it in Italy up to now. No, these things take time, and as far as I am concerned, the Marxist movement and what is taking place is moving fast enough from a historical point of view.

"The Grandeur of Automation and the Folly of Satellites." Please, when we are finished, there are always some gentlemen who like to come here and, in addition to asking questions, express themselves. I shall be very happy to hear you as long as you don't take too long. Will somebody tell me what is the advantage to humanity, in the state in which it is at the present time, to be spending all this enormous amount of money and energy on going to the moon taking photographs of the other side of the moon? I tell you frankly, I have no sympathy whatever with it, absolutely none. And primarily because I know why they are doing it. They are not interested in what is going on on the moon at all. They are not interested in scientific discoveries as Galileo was and Newton was and Einstein was. These fellows are interested in improving and perfecting weapons of destruction. I am against it. Who is for it? There is a lot more to be done with scientific knowledge, discovery, industry and organization in the world today than to be carrying on these idiotic and dangerous games. (applause)

## Freud

The next point is "Science and Man." I do not want to speak here without dealing with psychoanalysis. At the beginning of the century, Freud made what is certainly one of the greatest discoveries about human nature that has ever been made. He unfolded the power of the unconscious, the instinctive desires and needs of the human organism. Great writers and great artists have always been aware of it by the peculiar instincts and insight that they have. And Freud could point to this one and that one and the other and show that they had known what he was talking about. But he first put it on a scientific basis.

Now Freud was a revolutionary. I don't want to go into the problem of the unconscious, that is to say, first the raw, naked desires of humanity, human beings as animals. And then, above the unconscious some disciplined section of the personality which keeps some sort of order (the ego); and still above that, what he calls the super ego (which is something like Kant's Reason), which is still beyond the ego. I do not know much about it—you will get that in any book on psychoanalysis, and a lot of magazines vulgarize it. But most of them don't say what Freud actually said. There are two things about Freud which all these people—most of them—leave, but they play the fool and write as much nonsense about Freud as all these liberals and semi-socialists do with Marx. Freud taught infantile sexuality, the sexual instincts of the infant from the time it is born til it is about five or six years, that decides its character for the rest of its life. He is not playing. And number two, the neurosis, i.e., the incapacity of man to adjust himself—these instincts, despite ego and super ego—to modern or to any society, which makes neurosis a permanent feature of human character. Man cannot adjust himself to society. He is and must be psychologically sick. That is the true Freud.

Freud taught that if some people are very ill, half-crazy, they can be cured. He never set out to cure the whole world of a permanent neurosis. But most of the psychoanalyst practitioners, particularly in America, set out to cure every- and anybody. If you get into trouble with an American who is an intellectual, one question you ask him: who is your psychoanalyst? He will be very embarrassed, or he will tell you straightaway, and you and he are friends. (laughter)

## The Crisis of the Individual

As I see it, Freud's theory is the most merciless condemnation of society that you could think of. He said, "Human beings cannot adjust themselves to it. Absolutely impossible. The very sick ones I can cure. They have a disease. But the normal conditions of humankind, man being what he is, is a universal neurosis—inability to adapt himself to society." That is Freud. Anything else you read (one of the most offensive of all is a women in Hollywood; she makes a lot of money—all those movie stars go and lie down and tell her their troubles and she tells them something; they go off comforted and come back next time, paying a lot of money—she writes books telling how all can be adjusted), all that has nothing in common with Freud.

I have written one or two pages on Freud in a book of mine, and I sent it to the Psychoanalytic Society in the United States, and they sent it back to me next post. They will have nothing to do with it. They are out to cure people, you see, and I am quite sure that they can't cure them.

Yet I think there is a connection between Freud and socialism. I believe that we have reached a stage in modern society—I will not belabor the point—with a total reorganization of the fundamental economic basis of society which will itself involve, not today or tomorrow or the day after, but in the process of time, a reconstitution of sexual relations and the position of the women in society; a reconstitution of racial relations, because race prejudice is not got rid of very easily, you know; a reconstitution of class relations; the opportunity for the artist to work on the scale that the great artists of the past have worked and not to be faced continually with nothing else but signs of degeneration and demoralization, which they write for the public to read. I am not sure, but I believe that when Freud wrote as he did, he was conscious of society *as it was* and he meant that mankind would never be able to adjust himself to *this* society. Freud was no socialist. But in a socialist society, the unconscious could be the source of enormous power in the way human beings will tackle their social, and not only their individual, problems and not be the cause of a permanent neurosis. That is what I think. I think I understand what Freud was after, but I think his conception of society was too limited. He had no vision of a different type of society, and that is why he was so categorical. And to the extent that he was categorical in relation to bourgeois society, he was right.

This, of course, is very tentative. But I mention it because, though Marxism rests on economic relations, it is not confined to these, but opens up immense possibilities for the future development of society.

I had intended to say a few words about Jung. But there is no time, and in any case there is no need. Jung has made important discoveries, but his special theory of the "collective unconscious" means less to me every time I read it. Freud in particular demands a knowledge of medicine and even of therapy, but I have tested Jung's theory of the "collective unconscious" in regard to literature, and it seems to me a lot of nonsense and quite unnecessary nonsense.

And now we have finally "The Ascent of Man to Complete Humanity or Degeneration into the Life of the Cave and the Jungle."

The life of the cave and the jungle, I will not spend any particular time on; we know all about that. Twelve H-bombs (that was three or four years ago) could destroy civilized life in Britain. I think now with the great "progress" they are making, they could do it with three or four and, God willing, if the progress continues, they will be able to do it with one. No doubt in time they shall arrive at being able to destroy the whole big world with one little bomb. That would not end it. The struggle for the moon is on, to get it or destroy it if the other fellow gets it first. Possibilities are unlimited. Why not, after the moon, the sun? Not to destroy it, but to prevent it shining on the other half?

## A Review

I want to spend the last few minutes—it is ten minutes to ten—in giving you a brief view of how I see the world of yesterday, today and tomorrow: "The Ascent of Man to Complete Humanity." I hope you will bear with me. I am very happy with writers who continually review the situation and take up again what has already been covered.

We began with the Greek City-State, which Picasso has reminded us so forcibly of and so splendidly. The Greek City-States declined, and we had the Roman Empire. (I do not speak about the Jews because I do not wish to speak about religion. It makes a lot of trouble and it does not help. This is not the place; there are a lot of churches everywhere.) The Roman Empire gave Europe a sense of the unity of humanity. When Christianity came, it established that men were equal, if not in the world, in the sight of God. It was a form of equality. When the Roman Empire collapsed, the Roman Catholic Church took its place and for many centuries the Roman Catholic Church was not only the vanguard of religion, but it was the vanguard of civilization and gave Europe an even stronger sense of the unity of its intellectual, religious and to some extent its agricultural life. The church at one time was the most advanced practitioner both of agriculture and to some degree of industry. The unity of Europe as a concept in the consciousness of people was established first by the Roman Empire and secondly by the Roman Catholic Church which succeeded it. Then we have the Middle Ages and those workers in the towns that I have told you of. Here is the French historian, Boissonnade. He has written a fine book on San Domingo, a most respectable professor, and his book has been translated by Miss Eileen Power, formerly an equally respectable professor of medieval life and history in the London School of Economics. You will pardon me if I inflict upon you one of the finest passages that I know in history, a history of labor in the Middle Ages, of those towns—Florence, Ghent, Bruges, Antwerp, Siena, Rome and the rest of them. This is it:

*For the first time the masses, ceasing to be mere herds without rights or thoughts of their own, became associations of freemen* [this is the fifteenth century], *proud of their independence, conscious of the value and dignity of their labor, fitted by their intelligent activity to collaborate in all spheres, political, economic, and social, in the tasks which the aristocracies believed themselves alone able to fulfill. Not only was the power of production multiplied a hundredfold by their efforts, but society was regenerated by the incessant influx of new and vigorous blood. Social selection was henceforth better assured. It was thanks to the devotion and spirit of these medieval masses that the nations became conscious of themselves, for it was they who brought about the triumph of national patriotism, just as their local patriotism had burned for town or village in the past. The martyrdom of a peasant girl from the marshes of Lorraine saved the first of the great nations, France, which had become the most brilliant home of civilization in the Middle Ages. They gave to the modern states their first armies, which were superior to those of feudal chivalry. Above all, it was they who prepared the advent of democracy and bequeathed to the laboring masses the instruments of their power, the principles of freedom and of association. Labor, of old despised and depreciated, became a power of incomparable force in the world, and its social value became increasingly recognized. It is from the Middle Ages that this capital evolution takes its date, and it is this which makes this period, so often misunderstood, and so full of a confused but singularly powerful activity, the most important in the universal history of labor before the great changes witnessed by the eighteenth and nineteenth centuries.*

## Religious Theory Used for Reactionary Purposes

These were workers, workers over six centuries ago, laying the foundations of our civilization. You see, I respect the working class.

To continue. We know in Britain of the seventeenth century out of the religious preoccupation came parliamentary democracy. In eighteenth-century France, out of the struggle for political equality came the socialism of Babeuf. We remember Kant's tremendous effort to make people realize the contributions that the mind had to make to the examinations of the objective world. Kant had learned from Rousseau and particularly his *Social Contract*. The men of the Age of Reason did wonderful work, but the work that Kant began, the German philosophers, ending with Hegel, completed. From all this came Marxism in 1848. Now let these modern people tell you that there is no fundamental or no believable theory of the progress of humanity. That is what they are saying today; you find it everywhere: man is born to original sin. They are not religious. They steal the doctrine of original sin for political purposes. It is false.

There has been a development; the development is along the lines that I have tried to show. Man is ready for great strides forward today. But we have those two monstrous blocs; each of them has not only got enormous material power, but they have their labor movements—the democratic labor movements of Walter Reuther and the rest of them, and the Communist labor movement—and whichever way you turn they are waiting for you, either above with their diplomats and economic aid or below to catch you, each with his labor movement. In either case they have no other purpose but to involve you in their war preparations and their merciless struggle for world domination. I will not believe that this is the end.

## The Ascent of Man to Complete Humanity

In 1939 General Marshall and the American military authorities, aided by the government, organized fourteen million men and women. They washed them and dressed them and cleaned up their teeth and taught them to read, those who could not read. And then in two or three years they had them ready—for what? To go abroad, all over the world, fighting against people who had done the same thing on the opposite side. What is the purpose of these suicidal, these tremendous efforts on the part of human beings only to destroy one another? I believe it is possible to mobilize even more tens of millions of people for the work and the arts of peace. Properly encouraged and given a sense of history and a sense of destiny, they will do all they now do for war, for the sake of improving the normal life and relations of human beings. (applause) But this will come only when people are their own masters.

That for me is what Marxism is, and we must not be afraid, we must not think because we are small and insignificant that we are not able to take part in all that is taking place. The first thing is to know. Anyone who tries to prevent you from knowing, from learning anything, is an enemy, an enemy of freedom, of equality, of democracy. Those ideas, and the desire to make them real, have inspired men for countless centuries. Marxism is the doctrine which believes that freedom, equality, democracy are today possible for all mankind.

*If this course of lectures has stimulated you to pursue the further study of Marxism, we will have struck a blow for the emergence of mankind from the darkness into which capitalism has plunged the world.*

# Books to Read

A LONG LIST of BOOKS helps only professors and students. I would recommend here a few which you should have always by you.

*The Politics* of Aristotle in the edition of Sir Ernest Barker.

*The Social Contract* by Rousseau (Sir Ernest Barker's edition is pretty bad and should be avoided).

*The Communist Manifesto* by Karl Marx and Frederick Engels.

*Capital*, Volume 1, by Karl Marx.

*The State and Revolution* by V.I. Lenin, which now, I am informed, surpasses the Bible as the world's best-selling book

*The Acts of the Apostles* and *The Epistles of St. Paul*. St. Paul was a revolutionary advocating and organizing for a new revolutionary doctrine, Christianity. His writings give you a sense of history and the manner in which it moves.

For more modern studies, I recommend:

*Facing Reality* by Grace C. Lee, Pierre Chaulieu and C.L.R. James. This book gives as clearly as can be obtained within the covers of one small volume my own Marxist analysis of modern society.

*The Origins of Totalitarianism* by Hannah Arendt. Hannah Arendt does not understand the economic basis of society. But for knowledge and insight into the totalitarian monsters *and their relation to modern society*, her book is incomparably the best that has appeared in the post-war world.

All collections of documents on the Hungarian Revolution, such as *The Hungarian Revolution*, edited by Melvin J. Lasky.

# A Few Words with Hannah Arendt

ONE DOES NOT say everything every time one speaks or writes. To begin with, it is impossible, and there is no reason to argue further than that.

Yet in recommending as strongly as I do Hannah Arendt's book, I see an opportunity to supplement the view of Marxism which I have given in these lectures. In the latest edition of her book,[1] in a chapter on the Hungarian Revolution, Hannah Arendt says:

> For what happened here was something in which nobody any longer believed, if he ever had believed in it—neither the communists nor the anti-communists, and least of all those who, either without knowing or without caring about the price other people would have to pay, were talking about possibilities and duties of people to rebel against totalitarian terror. If there was ever such a thing as Rosa Luxemburg's "spontaneous revolution"—this sudden uprising of an oppressed people for the sake of freedom and hardly anything else, without the demoralizing chaos of military defeat preceding it, without coup d'état techniques, without a closely knit apparatus of organizers and conspirators, without the undermining propaganda of a revolutionary party, something, that is, which everybody, conservatives and liberals, radicals and revolutionists, had discarded as a noble dream—then we had the privilege to

1    Hannah Arendt, "Epilogue: Reflections on the Hungarian Revolution," chap. 14 in *The Origins of Totalitarianism*, 2nd ed. (Cleveland: World Publishing Company, 1958) 480–510; published in slightly different form as "Totalitarian Imperialism: Reflections on the Hungarian Revolution," *The Journal of Politics* 20, no. 1 (1958): 5–43.

witness it. Perhaps the Hungarian professor was right when he told the United Nations Commission: "It was unique in history, that the Hungarian revolution had no leaders. It was not organized; it was not centrally directed. The will for freedom was the moving force in every action."

Now, undoubtedly the large majority of political and other persons had given up hope of revolutionary upheavals to overcome totalitarianism and advance the socialist society (with the natural consequence that they put their hopes on A-bombs, H-bombs, etc.). But that everybody had given up hope is quite untrue.

In *Facing Reality*, published in 1958, the reader will see a full argument as to the inevitability of such upheavals. But this was after the revolution. In *State Capitalism and World Revolution*, first published in 1950 and then republished in 1957, the arguments are again stated. Let me, even at some cost of space, quote extensively.

You will find them in the periodical, *Correspondence*, which began publication in 1953.

You will find them also in the French periodical, *Socialisme ou Barbarie*, which began in 1948.

We did not have to wait until Stalin's death to foresee the crisis of Stalinism.

Here are our views as expressed in *State Capitalism and World Revolution*:

(c)  But the Stalinists are not proletarian revolutionists. They aim to get power by help, direct or indirect, of the Red Army and the protection of Russia and the Russian state. That is the reason why they follow the foreign policy of the Kremlin—it is sheer naked self-interest.

(d)  Theirs is a last desperate attempt under the guise of "socialism" and "planned economy" to reorganize the means of production without releasing the proletariat from wage-slavery. Historical viability they have none; for state-ownership multiplies every contradiction of capitalism. Antagonisms of an intensity and scope so far unknown already have Stalinism in their grip. Power merely brings these into the open.

The problem is of course a highly theoretical one.

We hope no one believes that the Stalinists go through all this merely for "Trotskyite-Bukharinist-fascists." To anyone who knows them and reads Leontiev's article, it is perfectly obvious that there is inside Russia itself a tendency to call Russia state-capitalism and the Stalinists can only fight it by mutilating *Capital*. They must attempt in theory as well as in practice to destroy every manifestation of the developing revolution in Russia. The theory of state-capitalism is the theoretical foundation for this revolution. . . .

The debate over Volume III of *Capital* is the debate over the developing revolution on a world scale and especially in Russia. If the problem is selling goods, then there is absolutely no economic reason for the collapse of the bureaucracy. If, however, the problem is the rate of surplus value in production, needed for expansion, then the bureaucracy is faced with a revolution in the process of production itself.

But great problems are solved by great forces. This is how we saw the solution of the problem in 1950: we did not have to wait for Hungary. For us, as Marxists, totalitarianism is doomed.

These intellectuals are the most cultivated in the modern world, in the sense of knowing the whole past of human culture. Having achieved what the idealism of Hegel posed as the Absolute, they are undergoing a theoretical disintegration without parallel in human history. In France this disintegration has assumed the form of a literary movement, Existentialism. In America it takes the form of a mania for psychoanalysis, reaching in to all layers of society but nowhere more than among the most urbane, sensitive and cultivated individuals. In Germany the intellectuals cannot choose between Christian Humanism and psychoanalysis, whether guilt or sickness is the root of the German catastrophe. This is total unreason, the disintegration of a society without values or perspective, the final climax to centuries of division of labor between the philosophers and the proletarians.

## Philosophy Must Become Proletarian

There is no longer any purely *philosophical* answer to all this. These philosophical questions, and very profound they are, Marxism says can be solved only by the revolutionary action of the proletariat and the masses. There is and can be no other answer. As we have said, we do not propose to do right what the Stalinists have failed to do or do wrong.

Progress in Russia, says Zhdanov, is criticism and self-criticism. The state owns the property, therefore the proletariat must work and work and work. The proletarian revolution alone will put state-property in its place.

In the United States the bourgeoisie extols all the advantages of democracy, the bureaucracy those of science. The proletarian revolution alone will put science in its place and establish complete democracy.

The evils that Christian Humanism sees, the problem of alienation, of mechanized existence, the alienated Existentialist, the alienated worker, internationalism, peace—all are ultimate problems and beyond the reach of any *ideological* solution.

The revolution, the mass proletarian revolution, the creativity of the masses, everything begins here. This is Reason today. The great philosophical problems have bogged down in the mire of Heidegger, Existentialism, psychoanalysis, or are brutally "planned" by the bureaucracies. They can be solved only in the revolutionary reason of the masses. This is what Lenin made into a universal as early as the 1905 Revolution: "The point is that it is precisely the revolutionary periods that are distinguished for their greater breadth, greater wealth, greater intelligence, greater and more systematic activity, greater audacity and vividness of historical creativeness, compared with periods of philistine, Cadet reformist progress."

He drove home the opposition between bourgeois reason and proletarian reason:

> But Mr. Blank and Co. picture it the other way about. They pass off poverty as historical-creative wealth. They regard the inactivity of the suppressed, downtrodden masses as the triumph of the "systematic" activity of the bureaucrats and the bourgeoisie. They shout about the disappearance of sense and reason, when the picking to pieces of parliamentary bills by all sorts of bureaucrats and liberal "penny-a-liners" gives way to a period of direct political activity by the "common people," who in their simple way directly and immediately destroy the organs of oppression of the people, seize power, appropriate for themselves what was considered to be the property of all sorts of plunderers of the people—in a word, precisely when the sense and reason of millions of downtrodden people is awakening, not only for reading books but for action, for living, human action, for historical creativeness. (*Selected Works*, Vol. VII, 261)

That was the first Russian Revolution. In the Second the proletariat created the form of its political and social rule. Now the whole development of the objective situation demands the fully liberated historical creativeness of the masses, their sense and reason, a new and higher organization of labour, new social ties, associated humanity. That is the solution to the problems of production and to the problems of philosophy. Philosophy must become proletarian.

I hope in future Hannah Arendt will not be so quick to say: all of us had given up hope. Those people who give up hope are those whose political ideas are not based upon the sense of history and philosophy which I have tried to establish in these lectures. The world today is full of political people who feel that they are caught in the trap of East bloc or West bloc, and even in many of the neutralists can be detected the sentiment that ultimately their fate lies with one or the other. Marxism has nothing in common with this fatalism or capitulation to seemingly all-powerful states.

## From Hungary to China

The appearance of the Workers Council in Hungary had a violent repercussion in Communist China. Here is an account of this based on careful examination of the Communist totalitarian press of China.

> The leaders in Peking immediately grasped the difference between the reformism of Gomulka and the revolution of the Hungarian Workers' Councils. If the Chinese press rushed to favour a policy which in Poland maintained the essentials of the bureaucratic structure while keeping a certain distance from Moscow, it just as rapidly interpreted the Hungarian revolt as a reactionary conspiracy plotted by the imperialists. But there had been too much abuse and epithets thrown against all kinds of people in China for the Chinese proletariat, itself struggling against the totalitarian regime, to accept the workers of Budapest, dying on the barricades, as fascist agents in the pay of the United States. From November 1956, despite the grossly deceitful character of the information spread in China, the advanced workers and students, often even members of the Party, perfectly understood what was taking place in Budapest. From that time on, the Hungarian Revolution acted like a powerful accelerator to the wave of opposition spreading across the length and breadth of China.
>
> Disturbed, the Chinese leaders took precautions. Conferences of security police were held one after the other. Everywhere the police were put on the alert, conspiracies were uncovered, and the accused confessed, as usual, that they were agents of Formosa.
>
> Despite this preventive terror, incidents multiplied at Shanghai in November. Opposition posters appeared in

the factories, streets and alleys of the old workers' quarters. Slogans were scratched on the walls and in the toilets. Mimeographed leaflets appeared. Beyond any question secret revolutionary nuclei existed. This campaign of agitation found its strongest echo among the masses. The factory workers and employees, to which were joined the unemployed and peasants who had fled the cooperatives, were creating "agitation and disturbances." Some demonstrations were organized, demanding a raise in wages, better living conditions, improved distribution in the market. Police spies were assassinated.

In the ensuing months strikes and demonstrations exploded in other areas of China. It was not surprising that in Kwantung, thirteen strikes accompanied by street demonstrations followed one another in quick succession during the course of the winter. In their turn the Peking and Manchurian areas were also centers of disturbances. In the mines of the Northeast the workers abused the doctors who refused to give them certificates of sick leave. The miners sat down at the bottom of the pits and refused to work.

In general, after coming to an agreement among themselves as to their demands, the workers began by sending letters and petitions to their leaders. Then they distributed leaflets, put up posters in the factories and on the streets. Sometimes they stopped work, noisily voiced their dissatisfaction and marched out into the streets where they provoked "all sorts of disturbances."

How did the forces of law and order react to these demonstrations? We do not have much information because the Chinese press is very discreet on this point. On June 10, 1957, however, a Peking publication will speak of the "machine guns which have been installed to suppress the disturbances," while an oppositionist will declare his certainty "that one day these machine guns will come back and fire in the opposite direction." Since autumn had the bureaucracy been machine-gunning down the workers? No one knows. But what is absolutely certain is that the police tried everything in order to disorganize the vanguard which had organized itself spontaneously in the factories and the mines. The official press supported them by vicious denunciations of the activities of "troublesome elements," "agitators," "anarchists."

The demands put forward by those "anarchists," however, were very elementary and often at the beginning specific to each factory. The strikers demanded better canteens, the installation of lavatories; sometimes they protested against the high cost of transportation, the bad housing conditions, and also, of course the inadequate wages and food. But their criticism soon took on more scope. They attacked the arbitrariness of the bureaucrats who managed the factories, the way that they distributed premiums and bonuses, and classified the personnel in the different professional categories. From there it was only a step to challenging the very principle of the bureaucratic management of the factory and the privileges of the apparatus. This was launched in Kwantung, that old bastion of the revolutionary proletariat, where the workers protested against the tremendous increase in salaries which the managing personnel was enjoying. They demanded democratic administration of the factories; the idea emerged that the leading bodies of the factory ought to be elected by the workers. Events moved quickly. In the spring the proletarian struggle was on the verge of placing in question the very foundations of the bureaucratic society.

Confronted with the mounting danger, the bureaucracy and the Party itself emerged as a much less solid bloc than it had been previously thought to be. In their turn the intelligentsia and the youth had been subjected to the shock of de-Stalinization and the Hungarian Revolution. Under the pressure of events, the apparatus began to crack. . . .

The Party had spared no efforts to build in the universities a new generation of cadres and technicians destined to take over gradually from the old layers impregnated with the ideological poisons of the old regime. The Chinese universities were like seminaries. Everything had been planned so that students would not have a single moment for reflection or personal reading. . . . But these factories for the manufacture of right-thinkers had produced a resounding reaction. The youth, rebelling against this tremendous machine to mold their brains, swung in the opposite direction and became madly romantic, rabidly individualistic.

After November a large section of the youth passed from romantic declamations and gestures to the political struggle. For many Party youth the Khrushchev report had been the springboard for a kind of thawing of their minds. The events in the fall only precipitated the debacle of their "totalitarian ideology." The Hungarian Revolution and in China itself the grumblings of the peasantry—disorders and strikes broke out at the beginning of winter in the villages—upset them further. In these circles, throughout November and December, there were passionate discussions of what had happened in Poland, in Hungary, and in China. In January it was clear beyond a shadow of a doubt that opposition currents had appeared among the young Party intellectuals which went far beyond official de-Stalinization and the demands for a liberalization of the bureaucratic dictatorship. Simultaneous with a similar development in the factories, a revolutionary vanguard was taking form among the intelligentsia.

Very quickly, in the light of what was taking place in China and the news from Budapest, these militants arrived at the conclusion that "the Party is the incarnation of bureaucratic despotism" and that "socialism can develop only on the foundations of direct democracy." For them the struggle of the Hungarian workers was a struggle "for the principle of direct democracy" and "all power should be transferred to the Workers Committees of Hungary." In the course of January the Party leaders were disturbed by what they called "the tendencies to anarchism" and to "extreme democracy." On January 25, an editorial writer in the official daily paper said how shocked he was by the ideas "professed by certain Party youth." One youth, the paper said, has defined democracy as follows: "On all matters, however important they may be, the masses must be able to vote. If the opinion of the masses is that a question ought to be resolved a certain way, the leadership then ought to resolve it in that way without any question." The theoretical magazine, *Hsue-Hsi*, on January 18 deplored that many youth "think that if you make state power the important factor in development and economic relations, then you cannot speak of communism. They believe that if socialist construction is directed by the state, then bureaucratic influences are inevitable."

... The decisive fact is that precisely at the moment when thousands of miles away Hungarian Workers Councils were being beaten into submission, the Chinese Communists of the younger generation had adopted as their own the essentials of the programme of the Hungarian Workers Councils.

Faced with this wave of agitation which was rising in the factories, villages, the universities, and beginning to decompose the totalitarian structure of the Party itself, the leading bodies hesitated and vacillated. In October and even in November the press denounced the activities as due to "counter-revolutionaries," "agents of Formosa," and of "the imperialists." The police suppressed the agitation, setting itself to the discovery of its leaders and the merciless destruction of the conspirators. But in December the official attack was already becoming more muted. The Peking leaders recognized the scope of the opposition and after what had happened in Budapest, they were careful not to repeat the mistakes of Gero and Farkas, afraid of ending up as these had. Thus the *People's Daily* will say "repression is a dangerous weapon because it not only cannot resolve the contradictions which are at the bottom of the disturbances but it can increase and aggravate them." Henceforth the workers' strikes, the growing agitation in the countryside, and the incidents in the universities are not only attributed to hidden "counter-revolutionaries." "Bureaucratism" is now blamed for all the evils that the nation is suffering. In January the turn is made. The middle and lower cadres are attacked with an extraordinary viciousness. There is no crime of which they have not been guilty: dictatorial methods, arrogance towards the masses, arbitrariness, incompetence, corruption, laziness. If the people are dissatisfied, it is because the true policy of the Party has been betrayed by those entrusted with carrying it out. In defiance of all the instructions they had been given, the cadres had shown "no concern for the sufferings of the people," had "stifled the opinions of the masses," and used their authority "to oppress the workers and violate their interests."

This aspect of Marxism I have not stressed in the lectures. But those who really want such information will find their way to it. The world will choose between hydrogen bombs and guided missiles, and some form of Workers Councils. In 1960, the Marxist doctrine: either socialism or barbarism, seems to me truer than ever before.

C.L.R. James

# About PMPress

politics • culture • art • fiction • music • film

PM Press was founded at the end of 2007 by a small collection of folks with decades of publishing, media, and organizing experience. PM Press co-conspirators have published and distributed hundreds of books, pamphlets, CDs, and DVDs. Members of PM have founded enduring book fairs, spearheaded victorious tenant organizing campaigns, and worked closely with bookstores, academic conferences, and even rock bands to deliver political and challenging ideas to all walks of life. We're old enough to know what we're doing and young enough to know what's at stake.

We seek to create radical and stimulating fiction and non-fiction books, pamphlets, T-shirts, visual and audio materials to entertain, educate and inspire you. We aim to distribute these through every available channel with every available technology — whether that means you are seeing anarchist classics at our bookfair stalls; reading our latest vegan cookbook at the café; downloading geeky fiction e-books; or digging new music and timely videos from our website.

Contact us for direct ordering and questions about all PM Press releases, as well as manuscript submissions, review copy requests, foreign rights sales, author interviews, to book an author for an event, and to have PM Press attend your bookfair:

**PM Press • PO Box 23912 • Oakland, CA 94623 • www.pmpress.org**

## FOPM  MONTHLY SUBSCRIPTION PROGRAM

These are indisputably momentous times—the financial system is melting down globally and the Empire is stumbling. Now more than ever there is a vital need for radical ideas. **Friends of PM** allows you to directly help impact, amplify, and revitalize the discourse and actions of radical writers, filmmakers, and artists. It provides us with a stable foundation from which we can build upon our early successes and provides a much-needed subsidy for the materials that can't necessarily pay their own way. You can help make that happen—and receive every new title automatically delivered to your door once a month—by joining as a Friend of PM Press. And, we'll throw in a free T-shirt when you sign up.

Here are your options:

- **$30 a month** Get all books and pamphlets plus 50% discount on all webstore purchases
- **$40 a month** Get all PM Press releases (including CDs and DVDs) plus 50% discount on all webstore purchases
- **$100 a month Superstar**—Everything plus PM merchandise, free downloads, and 50% discount on all webstore purchases

For those who can't afford $30 or more a month, we're introducing *Sustainer Rates* at $15, $10 and $5. Sustainers get a free PM Press T-shirt and a 50% discount on all purchases from our website.

Your Visa or Mastercard will be billed once a month, until you tell us to stop. Or until our efforts succeed in bringing the revolution around. Or the financial meltdown of Capital makes plastic redundant. Whichever comes first.

# A New Notion

Two Works by C.L.R. James:
"Every Cook Can Govern"
and "The Invading Socialist
Society"
C.L.R. James
Edited by Noel Ignatiev
$16.95 • 160 Pages
ISBN: 978-1-60486-047-4

C.L.R. James was a leading figure in the independence movement in the West Indies, and the black and working-class movements in both Britain and the United States. As a major contributor to Marxist and revolutionary theory, his project was to discover, document, and elaborate the aspects of working-class activity that constitute the revolution in today's world. In this volume, Noel Ignatiev, author of *How the Irish Became White*, provides an extensive introduction to James' life and thought, before presenting two critical works that together illustrate the tremendous breadth and depth of James' worldview.

"The Invading Socialist Society," for James the fundamental document of his political tendency, shows clearly the power of James' political acumen and its relevance in today's world with a clarity of analysis that anticipated future events to a remarkable extent. "Every Cook Can Govern," is a short and eminently readable piece counterpoising direct with representative democracy, and getting to the heart of how we should relate to one another. Together these two works represent the principal themes that run through James's life: implacable hostility toward all "condescending saviors" of the working class, and undying faith in the power of ordinary people to build a new world.

## A History of Pan-African Revolt

C.L.R. James
Introduction by Robin D.G. Kelley
$16.95 • 160 pages
ISBN: 978-1-60486-095-5

Originally published in England in 1938 (the same year as his magnum opus *The Black Jacobins*) and expanded in 1969, this work remains the classic account of global black resistance. Robin D.G. Kelley's substantial introduction contextualizes the work in the history and ferment of the times, and explores its ongoing relevance today.

"*A History of Pan-African Revolt* is one of those rare books that continues to strike a chord of urgency, even half a century after it was first published. Time and time again, its lessons have proven to be valuable and relevant for understanding liberation movements in Africa and the diaspora. Each generation who has had the opportunity to read this small book finds new insights, new lessons, new visions for their own age. . . . No piece of literature can substitute for a crystal ball, and only religious fundamentalists believe that a book can provide comprehensive answers to all questions. But if nothing else, *A History of Pan-African Revolt* leaves us with two incontrovertible facts. First, as long as black people are denied freedom, humanity and a decent standard of living, they will continue to revolt. Second, unless these revolts involve the ordinary masses and take place on their own terms, they have no hope of succeeding."
    —Robin D.G. Kelley, from the Introduction

"I wish my readers to understand the history of Pan-African Revolt. They fought, they suffered—they are still fighting. Once we understand that, we can tackle our problems with the necessary mental equilibrium."
    —C.L.R. James

## STATE CAPITALISM AND WORLD REVOLUTION

C.L.R. James,
Raya Dunayevskaya,
and Grace Lee Boggs
Introduction by Paul Buhle
Preface by Martin Glaberman
$16.95 • 160 pages
ISBN: 978-1-60486-092-4

Over sixty years ago, C.L.R. James and a small circle of collaborators making up the radical left Johnson-Forest Tendency reached the conclusion that there was no true socialist society existing anywhere in the world. Written in collaboration with Raya Dunayevskaya and Grace Lee Boggs, this is another pioneering critique of Lenin and Trotsky, and reclamation of Marx, from the West Indian scholar and activist, C.L.R. James. Originally published in 1950, this definitive edition includes the original preface from Martin Glaberman to the third edition, C.L.R. James' original introductions to three previous editions and a new introduction from James' biographer Paul Buhle.

"When one looks back over the last twenty years to those men who were most far-sighted, who first began to tease out the muddle of ideology in our times, who were at the same time Marxists with a hard theoretical basis, and close students of society, humanists with a tremendous response to and understanding of human culture, Comrade James is one of the first one thinks of."
   —E.P. Thompson

"C.L.R. James is one of those rare individuals whom history proves right."
   —*Race Today*

"It remains remarkable how far ahead of his time he was on so many issues."
   —*New Society*

## SEX, RACE, AND CLASS— THE PERSPECTIVE OF WINNING A SELECTION OF WRITINGS 1952–2011

Selma James
With a foreword by Marcus Rediker and an introduction by Nina López
$20.00 • 320 pages
ISBN: 978-1-60486-454-0

In 1972 Selma James set out a new political perspective. Her starting point was the millions of unwaged women who, working in the home and on the land, were not seen as "workers" and their struggles viewed as outside of the class struggle. Based on her political training in the Johnson-Forest Tendency, founded by her late husband C.L.R. James, on movement experience South and North, and on a respectful study of Marx, she redefined the working class to include sectors previously dismissed as "marginal."

For James, the class struggle presents itself as the conflict between the reproduction and survival of the human race, and the domination of the market with its exploitation, wars, and ecological devastation. She sums up her strategy for change as "Invest in Caring not Killing." This selection, spanning six decades, traces the development of this perspective in the course of building an international campaigning network. It includes excerpts from the classic *The Power of Women and the Subversion of the Community*, the exciting "Hookers in the House of the Lord," an incisive review of the C.L.R. James masterpiece *The Black Jacobins*, the groundbreaking "Marx and Feminism," and more.

"It's time to acknowledge James's path-breaking analysis: from 1972 she reinterpreted the capitalist economy to show that it rests on the usually invisible unwaged caring work of women."
    — Dr. Peggy Antrobus, feminist, author of *The Global Women's Movement: Origins, Issues and Strategies*